YASSARNAL QUR'AN

EASY TO LEARN QUR'ÂN

Rhythmic Method of
Learning Qur'ânic Arabic

With

English Pronunciations and important Du'as

Compiled & Edited by
Dr. Mohammad Noman Khan

Islamic Book Service

YASSARNAL QUR'ÂN

Compiled & Edited by: Dr. Mohammad Noman Khan

ISBN: 81-7231-492-2

1st Edition - 2003

Reprint Edition - 2005

Published by *Abdul Naeem* for

Islamic Book Service

2872, Kucha Chelan, Darya Ganj, New Delhi-110 002 (INDIA)
Ph.: 23253514, 23286551, 55360867, Fax: 23277913
E-mail: islamic@eth.net & ibsdelhi@del2.vsnl.net.in
Website: www.islamic-india.com

Our Associates

Islamic Book Service Inc.

136, Charlotte Ave., Hicksville, N.Y. 11801.
Ph.: 516-870-0427, Fax: 516-870-0429,
Toll Free # 866-242-4IBS
E-mail: sales@islamicbookservices.com
        ibsny@conversent.net

Al Munna Book Shop Ltd.

P.O. Box-3449, **Sharjah** (U.A.E.), Tel.: 06-561-5483, 06-561-4650
E-mail: nusrat@emirates.net.ae
Dubai Branch: Tel.: 04-352-9294

Printed at: *Noida Printing Press,* C-31, Sector-7, Noida (Ghaziabad) U.P.

Contents

بِسْمِ اللّٰهِ الرَّحْمٰنِ الرَّحِيْمِ

LEARNING QUR'ÂN

The tradition of teaching and learning Qur'ân has been continuing for a long time. There is a huge gap in the number of Arabic-speaking people and followers of Islam. A large number of Muslims are non-Arabic. So it is not possible for every Muslim to learn Arabic. But being a Muslim, it is his desire to read the Qur'ân. So anywhere there are Muslims, Qur'ân-reading people are there. That is why, Muslims of every language have tried to teach the alphabets of the Qur'ân in their language. Therefore, this tradition has been prevailing in this sub-continent since long time. A large number of **Qaidâs** have been prepared to teach the Qur'ân. This book is also an attempt in the same direction.

The intricacies of the Qur'ânic alphabets have been taught in a simple way for those who want to learn the Qur'ân. Exercises have been included as per the basis of latest mode of education so that the learner should not use only for cramming but also use his mind to make it more sharp..

There is a thorough discussion on **Makhârij** words so that he may know about **Makhârij** though without excercises, it is not impossible but also not easy.

In this Qaida different **du'as**, and **azâns**, have been included. Some small **sûrahs** have also been included so that they may be remembered before starting the learning of the Qur'ân. These will also be helpful in learning **namâz** and reading the Qur'ân. May Allâh make it helpful for us!

Though every effort has been made to make this Qaida perfect in every respect yet of readers find any shortcomings, the same may please be brought to the notice of the publisher so that those can be removed in the next edition if found justified.

—Dr. Mohammad Noman Khan

Pronouncing
THE ARABIC ALPHABET

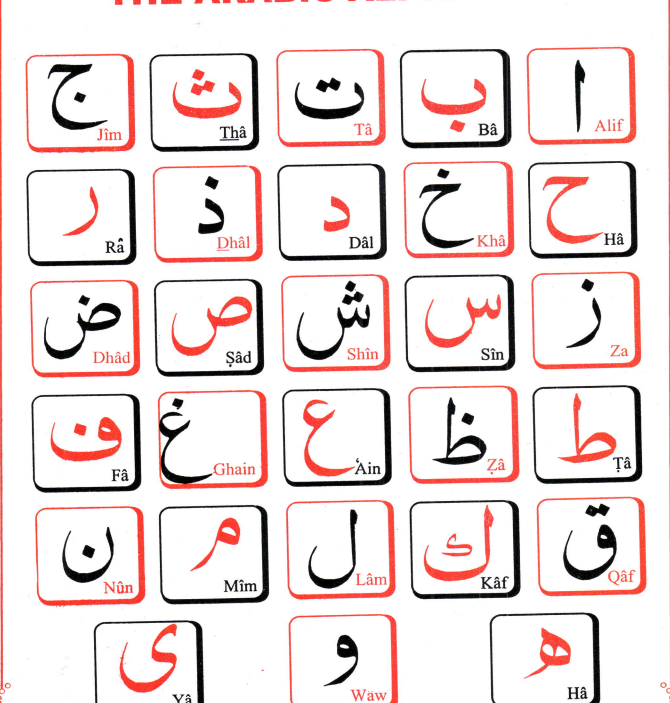

EXERCISES مشق

1. Learn by Heart: زبانی یاد کرو۔

ا ب ت ث ج ح خ د ذ ر ز س

ش ص ض ط ظ ع غ ف ق ك

ل م ن و ه لا ء ی

2. (i) Identify these letters: ان حروف کی پہچان کرو:

ا ب س ث ش د ذ ر ل ظ ن

ص ط ع ل ن و ه ی ء ت لا ق

غ ج ح ف خ ض ط ك م ء ن و

(ii)

ب غ ط س ص د ن ل م ث

ح خ ذ ض ظ ع ق ن ا

ء ی ت ج ك ش ا ر ه ے

مخلوط مشق
MIXED EXERCISE

ا ب ا ب ب ب ا ب ت ب ت ب

ث ت ث ث ت ت ج ت ب ت ث ت ج ح

خ ح خ ح ذ ذ خ د ذ ح د ح خ د

ر س ش ص ض س س ض ص ض س ز ش

ر ص ض ط ظ ط ظ ط ض ظ ط ع غ

ع ع غ ط ظ غ ع غ ف ق ك ك

ف ف ق ك ل م ر م ل م ن ن ل

ن و ه و ه ه لا لا ه لا ه ع و

ى ن ى ع ع و ى ى ع ى

7

LEARNING VOWELS

BASIC VOWELS	(HARAKAT)		حرکت
Fathah	(*Zabar*)	ـَ	زبر
Kasrah	(*Zer*)	ـِ	زیر
Dhammah	(*Pesh*)	ـُ	پیش
Sukûn		ـْ	سکون

NUNATION	(TANWEEN)		تنوین
Fathatain		ـً	
Kasratain		ـٍ	
Dhammatain		ـٌ	

SHADDAH	(TASHDEED)	ـّ	تشدید

MADDAH	ـٰا	ـٰ	ـٓ
	آ		

Short Maddah	ـٓ
Long Maddah	ـٓ

حرکات BASIC VOWELS

Arabic Alphabet with _Fatha_   (زَبر   _Zabar_)

Fatha is indicated by a small stroke (_ﹷ_) above the letter and pronounced like the 'u' in 'Bun'. It is also like a short 'a'. The letter which has _Fatha_ is called _Maftooh_.

فتحہ : زَبر دے ہ کو کہتے ہیں اور جس حرف پر زَبر ہو اُسے مفتوح کہتے ہیں۔

أَ بَ تَ ثَ جَ حَ خَ دَ ذَ رَ زَ

سَ شَ صَ ضَ طَ ظَ عَ غَ

فَ قَ كَ لَ مَ نَ وَ هَ یَ

EXERCISES

1.   Identify These Letters: ان حروف کی پہچان کرو۔

أَ بَ طَ عَ غَ دَ وَ هَ صَ شَ مَ ضَ

قَ هَ لكَ ظَ خَ نَ طَ یَ فَ نَ

2.   Read :   پڑھو۔

سَ لَ مَ دَ نَ قَ جَ رَب عَ مَلَ مَرَض

ضَ رَب وَ زَن دَ رَسَ وَ رَثَ

ARABIC ALPHABET WITH KASRAH

Kasrah is indicated by a small stroke (◌ِ) under the letter and pronounced like the 'i' in 'fig'. The letter which has a *Kasrah* is called *Maksoor*.

کسرہ : زیر (◌ِ) کو کہتے ہیں اور جس حرف کے نیچے زیر ہو سکتا ہو اسکو مکسور کہتے ہیں۔

اِ بِ تِ ثِ جِ حِ خِ دِ ذِ رِ زِ

سِ شِ صِ ضِ طِ ظِ عِ غِ فِ

قِ كِ لِ مِ نِ وِ هِ یِ

EXERCISES

1. Identify These Letters :

اِن حروف کی پہچان کرو۔

بِ تِ ثِ جِ حِ خِ زِ رِ فِ هِ یِ

وِ دِ ذِ نِ قِ كِ لِ اِ جِ عِ

غِ سِ شِ طِ ظِ صِ ضِ مِ

2. Read:

پڑھو۔

اِبِلِ   فِلِمِ   سِدِفِ   شِخِرِ

جِبِفِ   ثِتِرِ   مِرِدِ   رِازِقِ

وِزِنِ   اِبِلِ

10

ARABIC ALPHABET WITH DHAMMAH (Pesh پیش)

Dhammah is indicated by a small waw above the letter (ـُ) and is pronounced like the 'u' in 'pull'. The letter which has *Dhammah* is called *Madhmûm*.

ضَمَّہ پیش (ـُ) کو کہتے ہیں اور جس حرف پر پیش ہو اسے مضموم کہتے ہیں۔

اُ بُ تُ ثُ جُ حُ خُ دُ ذُ رُ

نُ سُ شُ صُ ضُ طُ ظُ عُ غُ

فُ قُ كُ لُ مُ نُ وُ هُ یُ

Identify These Letters: ان حروف کی پہچان کرو۔

بُ تُ ثُ حُ خُ رُ نُ فُ ہُ

یُ طُ ظُ دُ ذُ مُ وُ كُ لُ اُ

جُ نُ قُ عُ غُ سُ شُ صُ ضُ

Read: پڑھو۔

اُبُلُ مُرُدُ جُرُفُ سُرُفُ

شُخُذُ فُلُمُ نُرُفُ مُرُضُ

رُتُثُ اُبُلُ اُبُلُ

11

مخلوط مشق

MIXED EXERCISE

Read Carefully: ــ دھیان سے پڑھو

1.

دُ كَيْ كِيْ دُ خُ حُ جُ ثُ تِ تُ بُ اُ

قُ فُ غِ عُ ظُ طُ ضُ صُ شِ سُ

ئِ ءُ لّا هِ وُ نُ رُ مُ لِ كِ

2.

فَعَلَ فَرَضَ وَرَشَ سَرَشَدَ دَرَسَ

عَنِب حَبَرِ شَخِدَ فِلِمُ اِبَلِ

عُنْب سُطُرُ جُرُفَ فُلُمُ اَبُلُ

3.

كَتِب ضُرِب قَتَلَ نُصِرَ

حَنِف كَثُرُ كَثَدُرُ عَلِمَرَ

اُمَلَ اُسِرَ نُضِلَ مُثِلُ

TANWEEN (NUNATION) تنوین

At the end of Nouns, the vowel signs are written double as ‒‒‒, ‒‒‒, ‒‒‒. It means that they are to be pronounced with the final 'n'.

تنوین، دوپیش (ٌ)، دوزبر (ً) اوردوزیر (ٍ) کو تنوین کہتے ہیں یہ اسم کے آخرمیں آتی ہے۔

Arabic Alphabet with Fathatain (‒‒‒) دوزبر
Double Fathah (Fathatain) ‒ (‒‒‒) دوزبر

$$ اً = ً + ا \qquad بً = ً + ب $$

Alif + Double Fathah = An , **Bâ + Double Fathah = Ban**

Tan تً **Than** ثً **Jan** جً **Han** حً **Dan....** دً ....

أً بً تً ثً جً حً خً دً ذً رً زً

سً شً صً ضً طً ظً عً غً فً

قً كً لً مً نً وً هً یً

Identify These Letters: ان حروف کی پہچان کرو:

دً مً قً طً بً

جً زً سً فً شً لً هً غً

یً صً کً دً حً ذً عً تً

ضً ظً رً هً خً أً فً حً

13

ARABIC ALPHABET WITH KASRATAIN (ـــٍ)

Double Kasrah (Kasratain) ـٍ (ـــٍ) دو زیر

$$ اِ = ـٍ + ا \qquad بٍ = ـٍ + ب $$

Alif + Double Kasrah = In , **Bâ + Double Kasrah = Bin**

Tin تٍ Thin ثٍ Jin جٍ Hin حٍ Din.......دٍ

اِ بٍ تٍ ثٍ جٍ حٍ خٍ دٍ ذٍ

زٍ سٍ شٍ صٍ ضٍ طٍ ظٍ عٍ غٍ فٍ

قٍ كٍ لٍ مٍ نٍ وٍ ءٍ هٍ یٍ ےٍ

Identify These letters: ان حروف کی پہچان کرو۔

اِ نٍ بٍ خٍ جٍ دٍ ثٍ

حٍ شٍ ضٍ ظٍ غٍ كٍ قٍ فٍ

هٍ بٍ ءٍ یٍ صٍ عٍ مٍ تٍ

دٍ لٍ ذٍ وٍ طٍ فٍ لٍ جٍ

ARABIC ALPHABET WITH DHAMMATAIN (دوپیش ـوٗ)

Double Dhammah (Dhammatain) (دوپیش ـوٗ) ـٗ

بٌ = ـٌ + ب   اُ = ـٌ + ا

Bâ + Double Dhammah = Bun   **Alif + Double Dhammah = Un**

Dun......دٌ......   Hun حٌ   Jun جٌ   Thun ثٌ   Tun تٌ

اُ بٌ تٌ ثٌ جٌ حٌ خٌ دٌ ذٌ رٌ زٌ

سٌ شٌ صٌ ضٌ طٌ ظٌ عٌ غٌ فٌ قٌ

كٌ لٌ مٌ نٌ وٌ هٌ ءٌ یٌ ئٌ

Identify These letters: ان حروف کی پہچان کرو۔

دٌ مٌ سٌ شٌ ضٌ غٌ لٌ ذٌ رٌ

ذٌ بٌ نٌ قٌ جٌ حٌ مٌ دٌ هٌ

خٌ ءٌ یٌ فٌ عٌ طٌ ظٌ كٌ وٌ

MIXED EXERCISES OF TANWEEN

تنوین کی مخلوط مشقیں

1.

اً بٌ تٍ ثُ جٌ حٍ خٌ

دُ ذٌ رٍ زً سُ شٍ صُ

ضٌ طٍ ظُ عٌ غٍ فُ قٌ

كٍ لُ مً نٌ وٍ ءُ لاً ىُ

2.

اَ بَّ سَّ شَّ ثَّ دَّ رَّ

ذَّ ظَّ صَّ قَّ عَّ لَّ ةَّ

يَّ ضَّ طَّ ءَّ تَّ كَّ مَّ نَّ عَّ جَّ حَّ وَّ خَّ

3.

بِ مِّ ثِّ غِّ طِّ ضِّ سِّ خِّ حِّ

قِّ نِّ وِّ ذِّ ضِّ ظِّ فِّ لِّ عِّ جِّ

كِّ اِّ شِّ يِّ ىِّ تِّ

4.

اُ بُ طُ طُ عُ عُ دُ ذُ صُ شُ

مُ ضُ قُ كُ ظُ جُ زُ طُ ىُ

فُ نُ ءُ لُ ثُ تُ

5.

اِ بِ سِ ثِ شِ دِ لِ دِ

ذِ ظِ زِ صِ طِ عِ نِ لِ

وِ هِ ىِ ءِ تِ قِ غِ جِ

حِ فِ جِ ضِ طِ كِ مِ ءِ

نِ وِ

17

Vowellessness is called Sukûn(٥ ه) and a letter which has no vowel sign is called sâkin (a vowelless letter).

حرکت نہ ہونے کا نام سکون ہے اور جس حرف پر کوئی حرکت نہ ہو اُسے ساکن کہتے ہیں ۔

Sukûn with Fathah – with waw sâkin

اَوْ = اَ + وْ   بَوْ = بَ + وْ

Alif + waw sâkin = Aow   **Bâ + waw sâkin = Bao**

اَوْ	بَوْ	تَوْ	ثَوْ	جَوْ	حَوْ	خَوْ	دَوْ
ذَوْ	رَوْ	زَوْ	سَوْ	شَوْ	صَوْ	ضَوْ	طَوْ
ظَوْ	عَوْ	غَوْ	فَوْ	قَوْ	كَوْ	لَوْ	مَوْ
		نَوْ	وَوْ	هَوْ	ءَوْ	يَوْ

EXERCISE

خَوْف = خ ؕ + وْ + ف ؕ   لَمْ = لَ + مْ

فَوْج = فَ + وْ + ج ؕ   عَنْ = عَ + نْ

Sâkin with Kasrah (‎ـِـ) –
Ya Sâkin preceded by a letter with Kasrah

يَاسَاكِن مَاقَبْل كَسْرَه

إِىْ = اِ + ىْ

بِىْ = بِ + ىْ

Alif + Ya sâkin = Ee

Bâ + Ya sâkin = Bee

صِىْ	جِىْ	ثِىْ	تِىْ	بِىْ	اِىْ
سِىْ	زِىْ	رِىْ	ذِىْ	دِىْ	خِىْ
عِىْ	ظِىْ	طِىْ	ضِىْ	صِىْ	شِىْ
مِىْ	لِىْ	كِىْ	قِىْ	فِىْ	غِىْ
ىِىْ	ءِىْ	هِىْ	نِىْ	وِىْ	

A letter with sukûn preceded by a letter with kasrah

Sukûn with Kasrah

دِيْن = دِ + يْ + نْ

مِنْ = مِ + نْ

عِنْدَ = عِ + نْ + دَ

اِذْ = اِ + ذْ

19

Waw sâkin preceded by a letter with Dhammah

بُوْ = بُ + وْ

اُوْ = اُ + وْ

Alif + Waw sâkin = Oo

Bâ + Waw sâkin = Boo

حُوْ	جُوْ	ثُوْ	تُوْ	بُوْ	اُوْ
سُوْ	نُاوْ	رُوْ	ذُوْ	دُوْ	خُوْ
عُوْ	ظُوْ	طُوْ	ضُوْ	صُوْ	شُوْ
مُوْ	لُوْ	كُوْ	قُوْ	فُوْ	غُوْ
	يُوْ	ؤُوْ	هُوْ	وُوْ	نُوْ

A letter with sukûn preceded by a letter with Dhammah

Sukûn with Dhammah

قُلْ = قُ + لْ

جُوْع = جُ + وْ + ع

قُمْ = قُ + مْ

يُغْنِى = يُ + غْ + نِ + ى

SUKÛN PRACTICE

— **With Fatha**

طُمِسَت	طْ + مِ + سَ + ت	تْ	كَوْثَر	كَ + وْ = كَوْ	وْ
نَسَفَت	نُ + سِ + فَ + ت	تْ	بَيْتٍ	بَ + ىْ = بَىْ	ىْ

— **With Kasrah**

وَبِئْسَ	وَ + بِ + غْ + سَ	غْ	إِلَهْ	إِ + هْ = إِلَهْ	هْ
كَبِيرٍ	كَ + بِ + ىْ + رٍ	ىْ	مِنْ	مِ + نْ = مِنْ	نْ

— **With Dhamma**

تَمُوْرُ	تَ + مُ + وْ + رُ	وْ	قُلْ	قُ + لْ = قُلْ	لْ
غُرُوْرٌ	غُ + رُ + وْ + رُ	وْ	هُمْ	هُ + مْ = هُمْ	مْ

THE VOWEL FATHAH (◌َ) زَبَر

Name Fathah	Arabic Vowel ◌َ	Closest English Sound a
لَمُ = لَ + مُ		مَنْ = مَ + نْ مِنْهَا
عَبَسَ = عَ + بَ + سَ		خَتَمَ = خَ + تَ + مُ
أَغْطَشَ = أَ + غْ + طَ + شَ		أَسْفَلَ = أَ + سْ + فَ + لَ

21

THE VOWEL KASRAH (ـِ) زیر

Name	Arabic Vowel	Closest Eng. Sound
Kasrah	ـِ	i

مِنْ = نْ + مِ	فِیْ = یْ + فِ
بِحَمْدِ = دِ + مُ + حْ + بِ	ذِیْ = یْ + ذِ
سِرْفٍ + فِ + رْ + سِ	اِبِلٍ = لٍ + بِ + اِ

THE VOWEL DHAMMAH (ـُ و) پیش

Name	Arabic Vowel	Closest Eng. Sound
Dhammah	و	u

كُنْ = نْ + كُ	ثُمَّ = مَّ + ثُ
صُحُفٍ = فٍ + حُ + صُ	رَبِّكَ = كَ + بِّ + رَ
یَصُدُّ = دُّ + دُ + صُ + یَ	رَبُّكُمْ = مْ + كُ + بُّ + رَ

VOWEL PRACTICE

نَجْعَلِ = لِ + عْ + جْ + نَ	مَلِكِ = كِ + لِ + مَ
یَوْمَ = مَ + وْ + یَ	قُلْ = لْ + قُ
اِذْهَبْ = بْ + هَ + ذْ + اِ	اَحَدُّ = دُّ + حَ + اَ
مِرْصَادًا = دًا + ا + صْ + رَ + مِ	فَصِّلْ = لْ + صِّ + فَ

اَعْبُدُ = دُ + بُ + عْ + اَ

22

THE VOWEL NUNATION (ـٌ ـٍ ـً)

Name Nunation Symbol Closest Eng. Sound	Fathatain ـً an	Kasratain ـٍ in	Dhammatain ـٌ un

Fatha

| قَدْحًا = اح + دُ + قَ | اح | اَبَدًا = دَا + بَ + اَ | دًا |

Kasrah

| نَاصِرٍ = رَا + ص + ا + نَ | رٍ | نَفْسٍ = سٍ + فُ + نَ | سٍ |

Dhamma

| شَهِيدٌ = دٌ + ىْ + هِ + شَ | دٌ | فَصْلٌ = لٌ + صُ + فَ | لٌ |

Nunation Practice

مِرْصَادًا = دَا + ا + صَ + ثُ + مِ	دًا
سَبْعًا = ا + عً + بْ + سَ	عً
صُحُفٍ = فٍ + حُ + صُ	فٍ
حَاسِدٍ = دٍ + سِ + ا + حَ	دٍ
كُتُبٌ = بٌ + تُ + كُ	بٌ
وَيْلٌ = لٌ + ىْ + وَ	لٌ

23

THE VOWEL SHADDAH  DOUBLING OF LETTERS

The mark with three teeth is called *Shaddah*. (). It is a Symbol of assimilation of two same letters —first one *Sâkin* and second one with *Harakah* — into one letter e.g.

Shaddah with Fathah

خَ + نَّ + ا + سِ = خَتَّاسِ	ذَ + خَّ + تَّ + اِ = اِتَّخَذَ
تَ + بَّ + تُ = تَثَبَّتُ	رَ + نَ + بَّ + ا = رَبَّنَا

Shaddah with Kasrah

رَ + بِّ + كَ = رَبِّكَ	بِ + رَ + بِّ = بِرَبِّ
شَ + رِّ = شَرِّ	فَ + صَ + لِّ = فَصَلِّ

Shaddah with Dhammah

اُ + شَ + دُّ = أَشَدُّ	بِ + اَ + نَّ = بِأَنَّ
يَ + دُ + عُّ = يَدُعُّ	ىَ + ظُ + نَّ = يَظُنَّ

SHADDAH PRACTICE

With Fathah, Kasrah and Dhammah

EXERCISE–1

كَلَّا = ا + لَّ + كَ				ثُمَّ = مَّ + ثُ				
تَطَّلِعُ = عُ + لِ + طَّ + تَ				اَلَّتِی = ئ + تَ + لَّ + اَ				
حَمَّالَةَ = ةَ + لَ + ا + مَّ + حَ				حَمَّا = مَّ + ا + حَ				
تَوَّابًا = ا + بَّ + ا + وَّ + تَ				اِنَّهُ = هُ + نَّ + اِ				

فَحَدِّثُ = ثُ + دِّ + حَ + فَ				رَبِّكَ = كَ + بِّ + رَ			
فَصَلِّ = لِّ + صَ + فَ				سَبِّحْ = حْ + بِّ + سَ			
لِرَبِّكَ = كَ + بِّ + رَ + لِ				جَدِّكَ = كَ + دِّ + جَ			
رَتِّلُ = لُ + تِّ + رَ				فَسَبِّحْ = حْ + بِّ + سَ + فَ			

غَنِیٌّ = یٌّ + نِ + غَ				نَئیٌّ = ئیٌّ + نَ			
قَوِیٌّ = یٌّ + وِ + قَ				وَیٌّ = یٌّ + وَ			
یَاۤأَیُّهَا = ىَ + هُ + ىٌّ + أَ + ا + یَ				أَیٌّ = یٌّ + أَ			
یَدُعُّ = عُّ + دُ + ىَ				دُعُّ = عُّ + دُ			

EXERCISE-2

عَفَّ قَلَّ ضَلَّ حَجَّ وَدَّ جَدَّ حَدَّ اَدَّ

عَدَّ شَفَّ عَمَّ اَوَّ عَضَّ حَقَّ مَنَّ عَزَّ

اَىَّ خَفَّ بَثَّ اَنَّ شَتَّ

EXERCISE-3

كَرَّ ضَرَّ فَرَّ مَدَّ حَدَّ عَدَّ سَبَّ رَبَّ

جَلَّ فَلَّ بَلَّ فَلَّ رَدَّ جَدَّ مَرَّ حَرَّ

لَدَّ حَدَّ شَدَّ غَضَّ مَنَّ قَصَّ ظَلَّ ذَلَّ

صَبَّ حَبَّ عَسَّ دَسَّ

EXERCISE-4

اِلَّا مِمَّا جَدَّكَ سَبَّحَ اَنَّكَ حَرَّمَ رَبُّكَ

لِكِنَّ مِلَّةً حُجَّةً اَمَّةً لِلّٰهِ بِاللّٰهِ اِنَّكَ

مِنَّا عَدَّدَهُ عَذَّبَهُ قَبَّلَهُ قَرَّبَهُ اِنَّهُ عِزَّةً

EXERCISE-5

مَكَّنَّهُ لِلّٰهِ عَجَّلَ أَوَّلُ تَنَقَّبَّلَ أَضَلُّ إِيَّاكَ

حَيَّاكَ سَوَّكَ سَخَّرَ فَسَّرَ حَذَّرَ قُدَّرَ تَوَّابُ

أُذُنُ وَّ حُزْنُ وَّ أَرْضُ وَّ مُلْكُ وَّ خَلْقُ وَّ

EXERCISE-6

أَجْرُ مِّنْ نَصْرُ مِّنْ فَرِيْقٌ مِّنْ حَرْبُ مِّنْ

إِنْسُ وَّلَاجَانٌّ كَرِيْمٌ وَّمَاهُوَ تَنْزِيْلٌ مِّنْ عَزِيْزٌ مِّنْ

EXERCISE-7

صَوَّرَكُمْ سَخَّرَ لَكُمْ كَلَّا بَلْ تُحِبُّوْنَ قُدَّمَ وَاَخَّرَ وَالْتَفَّتِ

السَّاقُ بِالسَّاقِ فَلَاصَدَّقَ وَلَاصَلَّى وَلٰكِنْ كَذَّبَ

وَتَوَلَّى نُطْفَةً مِّنْ مَّنِيٍّ يُّمْنٰى بِالنَّفْسِ اللَّوَّامَةِ

27

LEARNING MADDAH SOUNDS

A maddah prolongs or lengthens vowel sound in the Qur'ânic script of Arabic

١	=	Doubles the length of a sound
～	=	Tripples the length of a sound
～	=	Five times the length of a sound

Most Qur'ânic scripts today do not differentiate between ____ & ____ They only use one generic ____. However in the principles of Tajweed there is guidance available about the differences in length

EXAMPLES OF SHORT MADDAH

Miniature Alif ___ and reverse Dhammah ___ .It occurs above or below a letter lengthening its sound to twice of the normal. It is like adding و ، ا or ی to that letter.

If it is a normal Fathah ___ , it is pronounced	= تَ
But with a miniature Alif above ___ , it is pronounced	= تَ
If it is a normal Kasrah ___ , it is pronounced	= بِ
But with a miniature Alif below ___ , it is pronounced	= بِ
If it is a normal Dhammah ___ , it is pronounced	= بُ
But with a reverse Dhammah ___ , it is pronounced	= بُ

PRACTICE OF SHORT MADDAH

ڭ ڭ ڭ	لُ لِ لَ	مُ مِ مَ	فُ فِ فَ
نُ نِ نَ	دُ دِ دَ	قُ قِ قَ	صُ صِ صَ
حُ حِ حَ	عُ عِ عَ	طُ طِ طَ	دُ دِ دَ
اُ اِ اَ	ذُ ذِ ذَ	تُ تِ تَ	غُ غِ غَ
شُ شِ شَ	خُ خِ خَ	بُ بِ بَ	جُ جِ جَ
سُ سِ سَ	یُ یِ یَ	ضُ ضِ ضَ	زُ زِ زَ
هُ هِ هَ	وُ وِ وَ	ثُ ثِ ثَ	ظُ ظِ ظَ

PRACTICE OF MADDAH

عٰبِدُوْنَ	يَاَيُّهَا	اَلنَّفّٰثٰتِ	اِلٰهَ
اَغْنٰى	يَدَآ	جَآءَ	اَلشِّتَآءِ
عَلٰى	اَلَّذِیْ	لِاِيْلٰفِ	سَيُصَلّٰى
بَنٰیَ	اِسْمُهٗ	اَلصّٰلِحٰتِ	يُرَآءُوْنَ
عِنْدَهٗ	اِنَّهٗ	اِنِّیَ	يَسْتَحْیٖ
فَذٰلِكَ	اَلْاِنْسَانَ	اَدْرٰىكَ	اِسْرَآئِيْلَ
اَلرَّحْمٰنِ	اَلضَّآلِّيْنَ	اَلْعٰلَمِيْنَ	اَعْطَيْنٰكَ

29

EXAMPLES OF LONG MADDAH

This Maddah always occurs above a letter prolonging its sound to three times or more. Compare in the examples given below how it interacts with other vowels on that letter.

Sound with Prolonged Fatha	Sound without prolonged Fatha	Sound with prolonged Kasrah	Sound without prolonged Kasrah	Sound with prolonged Dhammah	Sound without prolonged Dhammah
مَرْضَىٰٓ	مَرْضَىٰ	فِىٓ	فِى	قَالُوٓا	قَالُوا
اَنْزَلْنَآ	اَنْزَلْنَا	اِنِّىٓ	اِنِّى	اٰمَنُوٓا	اٰمَنُوا
اِنَّآ	اِنَّا	ثَمَرَةٓ	ثَمَرَةٖ	كَانُوٓا	كَانُوا

DIFFERENT MADDAH SOUNDS

In this exercise listen and try to differentiate between the

Length of the Maddah sounds

Pronounce these letters very well:

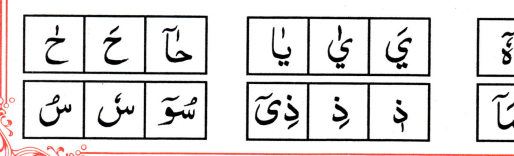

EXERCISE-1

فَهُوَيَرٰى مُوۡسٰى عِيۡسٰى هُدٰى بِالتَّقۡوٰى اِلٰى رَبِّكَ

الرُّجۡعٰى وَتَوَلّٰى اِذَاصَلّٰى خَيۡرٌلَّكَ مِنَ الۡاُوۡلٰى

وَالضُّحٰى وَالَّيۡلِ اِذَا سَجٰى فَاٰوٰى تُجۡزٰى رَبُّكَ فَتَرۡضٰى

EXERCISE-2

Exercise for Short Madda:

چھوٹی مَدّ کی مشق :

قَضٰۤى مُوۡسٰى يَعِيۡسٰى عَلٰۤى اَزۡوَاجِهِمۡ مَاهٰذَاۤ

مَاۤاٰتَوۡا قَالُوۡۤا ءَاِذَا مِثۡنَالَااِلٰهَ فِيۡهَا مَاكَانُوۡۤا

كَمَا لَوۡلَا سَتَجِدُنِۤیۡ عَجِبُوۡۤا اَنۡزَلۡنَاۤ

EXERCISE-3

Exercise for Long Madda:

بڑی مَدّ کی مشق :

عَلٰى نِسَآءِ الۡعَالَمِيۡنَ يَابَنِیۡۤ اِسۡرَآءِيۡلَ الٓمّٓ

اِلٰى كَلِمَةٍ سَوَآءٍ قَآئِمًا اُولٰٓئِكَ وَجَآءَهُمۡ ضِيَآءً

قَآئِمِيۡنَ طَآئِفِيۡنَ دِمَآءَهُمۡ حُنَفَآءَ شَعَآئِرُ

سَمَآءٌ شُهَدَآءُ

EXERCISES FOR  SOUNDS

EXERCISE-1

Pronounce correctly these words:

عَلٰى	هٰذَا	مَالَهُ	مَلِك
اِلٰهٌ	اَمَنَ	اَللّٰهُ	اِنَّهُ
اِمْرَاَتُهُ	سَيُصَلّٰى	يَبْنٰى	اَغْنٰى
اَلنَّفّٰثٰتِ	حَتّٰى	سُبْحٰانَهُ	دَاؤُدَ
اٰيٰتِهِ	اِسْمُهُ	اَلْفِهِمْ	عٰبِدُوْنَ

EXERCISE-2

قَ اَل ، قَالَ ، قُلَ ، مَ الِ ك ، مَالِك ،

مَلِك ، اٰدَمَ ، اٰمَنَ ، كِتَابٌ ، كُتُبٌ

سُبْحٰنَك سَمٰوٰتٍ كَلِمٰتٍ اِذَا اَرْهِم

مَاٰرِبُ رَءٰ قُنْهُمْ لِلْمَلٰٓئِكَةِ خَطٰيٰكُمْ

ذٰلِك جِءْنٰهُمْ يَبْنٰى يَحْيٰى

صَلٰوةٌ مَتٰى بِالْهُدٰى

32

ب سِ ىُٔ بِه ، ىُٔ خِ رِ ى ، تُحِيى

اِبرٰهمَ الفِهمُ تُرزقِنه وقِيله

وقِله ، يَستَحِى

بَعدِه لا يُلِف لِٔيلِف

ب مُ رَ حُ رِ ح ه ، مكلَ

بِمُ رَ حُ رِ ح ه ، مِن بَعدِه

LETTERS OF MUQATTA'ÂT
حروف مقطعات

The following are the unique combination of letters which occur in the beginning of some surahs of the Holy Qur'ân.

Each letter is pronounced separately according to the Maddah symbol on it. Children should be taught the pronunciation of these letters carefully:

بچّوں کو ان حروف کے تلفّظ اچھی طرح سمجھائیں :۔

طٰهٰ	الٓمّٓصٓ	الٓمّٓرٰا	الٓرٰا	الٓمّٓ
طَا ھَا	الف لَام مِيم صَاد	الف لَام مِيم رَا	الف لَام رَا	الف لَام مِيم
کٰهٰیٰعٓصٓ	عٓسٓقٓ	طٰسٓمّٓ	طٰسٓ	یٰسٓ
کَاف ھَا یَا عَین صَاد	عَین سَین قَاف	طَا سَین مِیم	طَا سَین	یَاسِین
	حٰمّٓ	نٓ	قٓ	صٓ
	حَا مِیم	نُون	قَاف	صَاد

Number of prostrations and chapters in the Holy Qur'ân:

قرآن پاک میں سجدات اور سورتوں کی تعداد ۔

سجدات تلاوت قرآن شریف میں چودہ پندرہ ہیں۔ سجدے والی آیت پڑھی جائے تو پڑھنے والے اور سننے والے دونوں پر سجدہ کرنا لازم ہو جاتا ہے۔ اگر جگہ نہ ملے یا بھول جائیں تو بعد میں ادا کریں۔ تمام قرآن مجید میں کل ایک سو چودہ سورتیں ہیں الحمد شریف کا نام سورۃ فاتحہ ہے۔

Prostrations (during reciting the Holy Qur'ân) are fourteen or fifteen in number. Performed immediately or later on. When an Ayah with Sajda (prostration) is recited, prostration becomes compulsory on both the readers and the listeners. There are One Hundred and Fourteen Chapters in the Holy Qur'ân in all. The name of the opening Chapter (Al-Hamd Shareef) is Surah-al-Fatiha.

نوٹ :۔ قرآن شریف کو بے وضو کبھی ہاتھ نہیں لگانا چاہیے۔ ہاں بے وضو پڑھنا جائز ہے۔ با وضو پڑھنے میں زیادہ ثواب ہے۔

Note: The Holy Qur'ân should never be touched without Wudu'. Reciting of Qur'ân without Wudu' is permissible, but if we read it with wudu', we will deserve more rewards from Allâh.

CONNECTING LETTERS

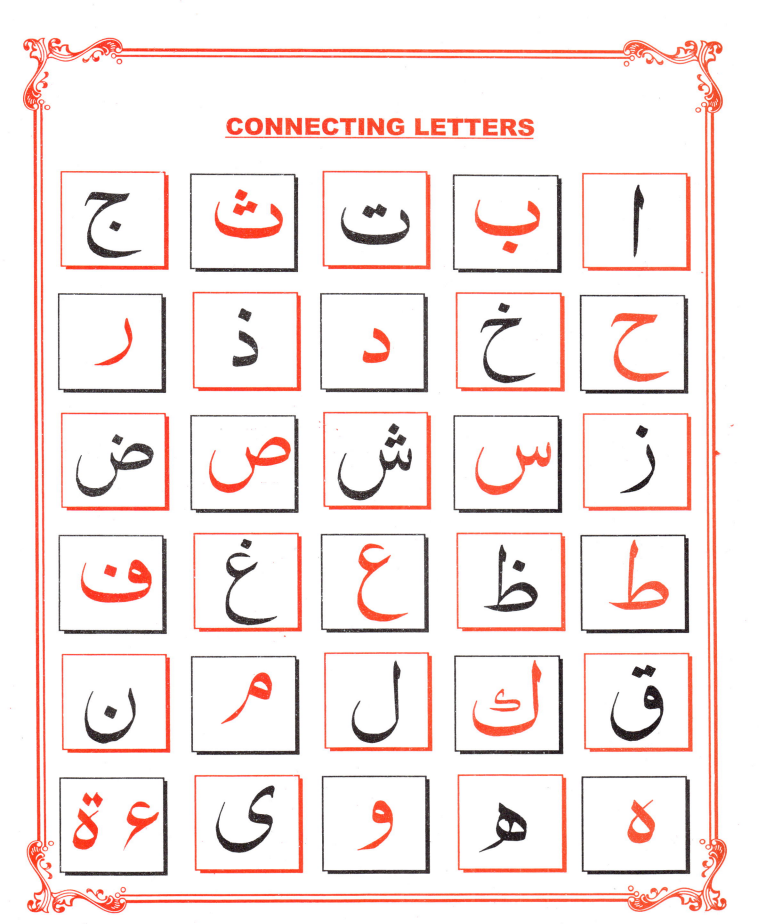

ALIF — ١

Ending	Middle	Beginning
١	١	١

English equivalent = a

Beginning:

أَ + لُ + لَ + ١ + هُ = اللهُ = بِسۡمِ اللهِ الرَّحۡمٰنِ الرَّحِيۡمِ۔
أَ + لَ + مُ = اَلَمُ = اَلَمۡ نَشۡرَحۡ لَكَ صَدۡرَكَ ۔
أَ + صُ + خ + بُ = أَصۡحٰبُ = قُتِلَ أَصۡحٰبُ الۡأُخۡدُوۡدِ۔

Middle:

غَ + ١ + سِ + قٍ = غَاسِقٍ = وَمِنۡ شَرِّ غَاسِقٍ اِذَا وَقَبَ۔
عَ + ذَ + ١ + بُ = عَذَابُ = وَلَهُمۡ عَذَابُ الۡحَرِيۡقِ ۔
یُ + حَ + ١ + سَ + بُ = یُحَاسَبُ = فَسَوۡفَ یُحَاسَبُ حِسَابًا یَّسِيۡرًا

Ending:

جِ + ىۡ + دِ + هَ + ١ = جِيۡدِهَا = فِیۡ جِيۡدِهَا حَبۡلٌ مِّنۡ مَّسَدٍ۔
عَ + لَ + ىۡ + نَ + ١ = عَلَيۡنَا = اِنَّ عَلَيۡنَا لَلۡهُدٰی۔
زِ + لُ + زَ + ١ + لَ + هَ + ١ = زِلۡزَالَهَا = اِذَا زُلۡزِلَتِ الۡأَرۡضُ زِلۡزَالَهَا۔

BÂ — ب

Ending	Middle	Beginning
بـ ـب	ـبـ	بـ

English equivalent= b

Beginning:

بِسْمِ اللّٰهِ الرَّحْمٰنِ الرَّحِيْمِ = بِسْمِ = مِ + سْ + بِ

فَسَبِّحْ بِحَمْدِ رَبِّكَ وَاسْتَغْفِرْهُ = بِحَمْدِ = دِ + مْ + حَ + بِ

وَتَوَاصَوْا بِالصَّبْرِ = بِالصَّ = رَ + بْ + صَّ + اَ + بِ

Middle:

تَبَّتْ يَدَاۤ اَبِىْ لَهَبٍ وَّتَبَّ = تَبَّتْ = تْ + بَّ + تَ

اِنَّ رَبَّهُمْ بِهِمْ يَوْمَئِذٍ لَّخَبِيْرٌ = رَبَّهُمْ = مْ + هُ + بَّ + رَ

بِاَنَّ رَبَّكَ اَوْحٰى لَهَا ۗ = رَبَّكَ = كَ + بَّ + رَ

Ending:

مَاۤ اَغْنٰى عَنْهُ مَالُهُ وَمَا كَسَبَ = كَسَبَ = بَ + سَ + كَ

اَرَءَيْتَ الَّذِىْ يُكَذِّبُ بِالدِّيْنِ = يُكَذِّبُ = بُ + ذِّ + كَ + يُ

فِيْهَا كُتُبٌ قَيِّمَةٌ = كُتُبٌ = بٌ + تُ + كُ

TÂ — ت

Ending	Middle	Beginning
ت ت	ـتـ	ت

English equivalent= t

Beginning:

ت + وَّ + ا + بًّ = تَوَّابًا = اِنَّهٗ كَانَ تَوَّابًا ۔
تَ + عۡ + لَ + مُ + وۡ + نَ = تَعۡلَمُوۡنَ = كَلَّا سَوۡفَ تَعۡلَمُوۡنَ ۔
تَ + طّ + لِ + عُ = تَطَّلِعُ = اَلَّتِیۡ تَطَّلِعُ عَلَی الۡاَفۡـِٔدَةِ ۔

Middle:

اَ + نۡ + ت + مُ = اَنۡتُمۡ = وَلَا اَنۡتُمۡ عَابِدُوۡنَ مَا اَعۡبُدُ ۔
لَ + تُ + سۡ + ءَ + لُ + نَّ = لَتُسۡـَٔلُنَّ = ثُمَّ لَتُسۡـَٔلُنَّ یَوۡمَئِذٍ عَنِ النَّعِیۡمِ
اَ + نۡ + ذَ + رۡ + تُ + كُ + مۡ = اَنۡذَرۡتُكُمۡ = فَاَنۡذَرۡتُكُمۡ نَارًا تَلَظّٰی ۔

Ending :

اَ + نۡ + عَ + مۡ + تَ = اَنۡعَمۡتَ = صِرَاطَ الَّذِیۡنَ اَنۡعَمۡتَ عَلَیۡهِمۡ
ثَ + قُ + لَ + تۡ = ثَقُلَتۡ = فَاَمَّا مَنۡ ثَقُلَتۡ مَوَازِیۡنُهٗ ۔
اَ + لۡ + بَ + یۡ + تِ = الۡبَیۡتِ = فَلۡیَعۡبُدُوۡا رَبَّ هٰذَا الۡبَیۡتِ ۔

THÂ – ث

Ending	Middle	Beginning
ث	ث	ش

English equivalent = th

Beginning:

ثَ + مَّ = ثُمَّ = كَلَّا سَوْفَ تَعْلَمُوْنَ ۔

ثَ + مُ + وْ + دُ = ثَمُوْدُ = كَذَّبَتْ ثَمُوْدُ بِطَغْوٰهَآ ۔

ثُ + وِّ + بَ = ثُوِّبَ = هَلْ ثُوِّبَ الْكُفَّارُ مَا كَانُوْا يَفْعَلُوْنَ ۔

Middle:

أَ + لْ + نَّ + فّ + ثّ + تِ = ألنَّفّٰثٰتِ = وَمِنْ شَرِّ النَّفّٰثٰتِ فِي الْعُقَدِ ۔

عُ + ثَ + آ + ءً = غُثَآءً = فَجَعَلَهُ غُثَآءً أَحْوٰى ۔

تُ + ؤْ + ثِ + رُ + وْ + نَ = تُؤْثِرُوْنَ = بَلْ تُؤْثِرُوْنَ الْحَيٰوةَ الدُّنْيَا ۔

Ending:

حَ + دِ + ىْ + ثُ = حَدِيْثُ = هَلْ أَتٰىكَ حَدِيْثُ الْغَاشِيَةِ ۔

بَ + عَ + ثَ = بَعَثَ = اِذَا انْبَعَثَ أَشْقٰهَا ۔

حَ + دِ + ىْ + ثُ = حَدِيْثُ = هَلْ أَتٰىكَ حَدِيْثُ الْجُنُوْدِ ۔

JÎM — ج

Ending	Middle	Beginning
جـ	ـجـ	ج

English equivalent= j

Beginning:

جَ + ـ = جَآءَ = عَ + آ	اِذَا جَآءَ نَصْرُ اللهِ وَالْفَتْحُ =			
جَ + حِ = جَحِيْمٍ = مٍ + ىْ + حِ	وَاِنَّ الْفُجَّارَ لَفِيْ جَحِيْمٍ ـ			
جَ + لَّ = جَلَّهَا = ا + هَ	وَالنَّهَارِ اِذَا جَلَّهَا ـ			

Middle:

اَ + لْ + جِ + نَّ + ةِ = اَلْجِنَّةِ = مِنَ الْجِنَّةِ وَالنَّاسِ ـ					
نُ + رِّ + جَ + تْ = نُرِّجَتْ = وَاِذَا النُّفُوْسُ زُوِّجَتْ ـ					
فُ + جِّ + تْ = فُجِّرَتْ = وَاِذَا الْبِحَارُ فُجِّرَتْ ـ					

Ending:

اَ + لْ + حَ + جّ = اَلْحَجّ = وَاَذِّنْ فِي النَّاسِ بِالْحَجّ ـ					
اَ + لْ + بُ + سُ + وْ + جِ = اَلْبُرُوْجِ = وَالسَّمَآءِ ذَاتِ الْبُرُوْجِ ـ					
اَ + خْ + سَ + جَ = اَخْرَجَ = وَالَّذِيْٓ اَخْرَجَ الْمَرْعَى ـ					

40

HÂ — ح

Ending	Middle	Beginning
حـ ـح	ـحـ	حـ

English equivalent= h

Beginning:

حَ + ا + سِ + دٍ = حَاسِدٍ = وَمِنْ شَرِّ حَاسِدٍ اِذَا حَسَدَ ۔
حَ + ا + فِ + ظٌ = حَافِظٌ = اِنْ كُلُّ نَفْسٍ لَّمَّا عَلَيْهَا حَافِظٌ
حِ + جْ + رٍ = حِجْرٍ = هَلْ فِىْ ذٰلِكَ قَسَمٌ لِّذِىْ حِجْرٍ ۔

Middle:

اَ + لْ + حَ + مْ + دُ = اَلْحَمْدُ = اَلْحَمْدُ لِلّٰهِ رَبِّ الْعٰلَمِيْنَ ۔
يَ + حُ + ضُّ = يَحُضُّ = وَلَا يَحُضُّ عَلٰى طَعَامِ الْمِسْكِيْنِ
صُ + حُ + فِ = صُحُفِ = صُحُفِ اِبْرَاهِيْمَ وَمُوْسٰى ۔

Ending:

فَ + سَ + بِّ + حْ = فَسَبِّحْ = فَسَبِّحْ بِحَمْدِ رَبِّكَ وَاسْتَغْفِرْهُ ۔
اَ + فْ + لَ + حَ = اَفْلَحَ = قَدْ اَفْلَحَ مَنْ زَكّٰهَا ۔
سَ + بِّ + حْ = سَبِّحْ = سَبِّحِ اسْمَ رَبِّكَ الْاَعْلٰى ۔

KHÂ – خ

Ending	Middle	Beginning
ـخ	ـخـ	خـ

English equivalent = kh

Beginning:

خَ + لَ + قَ = خَلَقَ = مِنْ شَرِّ مَا خَلَقَ ۔
خَ + ا + شِ + عَ + ةٌ = خَاشِعَةٌ = اَبْصَارُهَا خَاشِعَةٌ
خُ + لِ + قَ = خُلِقَ = خُلِقَ مِنْ مَّاءٍ دَافِقٍ ۔

Middle:

يَ + جْ + رُ + خْ + یُ = يَخْرُجُ = يَخْرُجُ مِنْ بُطُوْنِهَا شَرَابٌ ۔
اَ + لْ + خُ + نَّ + ا + سِ = اَلْخُنَّاسِ = مِنْ شَرِّ الْوَسْوَاسِ الْخَنَّاسِ ۔
نُ + خْ + رِ + جَ = نُخْرِجَ = لِنُخْرِجَ بِهٖ حَبًّا وَّ نَبَاتًا ۔

Ending:

نُ + فِ + خَ = نُفِخَ = فَاِذَا نُفِخَ فِي الصُّوْرِ ۔
نَ + سْ + لَ + خُ = نَسْلَخُ = نَسْلَخُ مِنْهُ النَّهَارَ ۔
صَ + رِ + يْ + خَ = صَرِيْخَ = فَلَا صَرِيْخَ لَهُمْ وَلَا هُمْ يُنْقَذُوْنَ ۔

DÂL — د

Ending	Middle	Beginning
ـد	ـدـ	د

English equivalent = d

Beginning:

دِ + يْ = دِيْنٍ = لَكُمْ دِيْنُكُمْ وَلِيَ دِيْنٍ ۔		نٍ +	يْ +	دِ +
دُ + وْ = دُوْنٍ = فَلَمْ يَجِدُوْا لَهُمْ مِّنْ دُوْنِ اللهِ أَنْصَارًا ۔		نٍ +	وْ +	دُ +
دَ + ا = دَانِ = وَجَنَا الْجَنَّتَيْنِ دَانٍ ۔		نِ +	ا +	دَ +

Middle:

تَعْبُدُوْنَ = لَا أَعْبُدُ مَا تَعْبُدُوْنَ ۔	نَ +	وْ +	دُ +	بُ +	عْ +	تَ +
وَاحِدَةٌ = نُفِخَ فِي الصُّوْرِ نَفْخَةٌ وَّاحِدَةٌ ۔	ةٌ +	دَ +	حِ +	ا +	وَ +
تَدْعُوْ = فَلَا تَدْعُوْا مَعَ اللهِ أَحَدًا ۔	وْ +	عُ +	دْ +	تَ +

Ending :

أَحَدٌ = قُلْ هُوَ اللهُ أَحَدٌ ۔	دٌ +	حَ +	أَ +
نَعْبُدُ = إِيَّاكَ نَعْبُدُ ۔	دُ +	بُ +	عْ +	نَ +
الصَّمَدُ = اَللهُ الصَّمَدُ ۔	دُ +	مَ +	صَّ +	لُ +	اَ +

43

DHÂL — ذ

Ending	Middle	Beginning
ذ	ـذ	ذ

English equivalent = dh

Beginning:

سَيَصْلَى نَارًا ذَاتَ لَهَبٍ ۔	ذَاتَ =	تَ +	ا +	ذَ	
ذٰلِكَ الْيَوْمُ الَّذِى كَانُوْا يُوْعَدُوْنَ ۔	ذٰلِكَ =	كَ +	لِ +	ا +	ذَ
فَمَنْ يَّعْمَلْ مِثْقَالَ ذَرَّةٍ خَيْرًا يَّرَهٗ ۔	ذَرَّةٍ =	ةٍ +	رَّ +	ذَ	

Middle:

صِرَاطَ الَّذِيْنَ اَنْعَمْتَ عَلَيْهِمْ	اَلَّذِيْنَ =	نَ +	ىْ +	ذِ +	لَّ + اَ
اَعَدَّ اللّٰهُ لَهُمْ عَذَابًا شَدِيْدًا ۔	عَذَابًا =	ا +	بَّ +	ا +	ذَ + عَ
وَلِلْكٰفِرِيْنَ عَذَابٌ اَلِيْمٌ ۔	عَذَابٌ =	بٌ +	ا +	ذَ + عَ

Ending:

ثُمَّ لَتُسْئَلُنَّ يَوْمَئِذٍ عَنِ النَّعِيْمِ ۔	يَوْمَئِذٍ =	ذٍ +	ءِ +	مَ +	وْ + ىَ
يٰيَحْيٰى خُذِ الْكِتٰبَ بِقُوَّةٍ ۔	خُذْ =	ذْ +	خُ		

RÂ – ر

Ending	Middle	Beginning
ـر	ـرـ	ر

English equivalent = r

Beginning:

رَ + بَّ = رَبَّ = فَلْيَعْبُدُوا رَبَّ هٰذَا الْبَيْتِ ـ
رَ + ضِ + ىٰ = رَضِىَ = رَضِيَ اللهُ عَنْهُمْ وَرَضُوا عَنْهُ ـ
رَ + اَ + ىْ + تَ + هُ + مْ = رَاَيْتَهُمْ = إِذَا رَاَيْتَهُمْ حَسِبْتَهُمْ لُؤْلُؤًا مَّنْثُورًا ـ

Middle:

اَ + ل + رَّ + حْ + مٰ + نِ = اَلرَّحْمٰنِ = اَلرَّحْمٰنِ الرَّحِيْمِ ـ
نَ + ضْ + رَ + ةً = نَضْرَةً = وَلَقّٰهُمْ نَضْرَةً وَّسُرُورًا ـ
اَ + لْ + اٰ + خِ + رَ + ةِ = اَلْاٰخِرَةِ = وَلَهُمْ فِي الْاٰخِرَةِ عَذَابُ النَّارِ ـ

Ending:

وَ + ا + نْ + حَ + رُ = وَانْحَرْ = فَصَلِّ لِرَبِّكَ وَانْحَرْ ـ
اَ + طْ + هَ + رُ = اَطْهَرُ = ذٰلِكَ خَيْرٌ لَّكُمْ وَاَطْهَرُ ـ
خَ + بِ + يْ + رُ = خَبِيْرُ = وَاللهُ بِمَا تَعْمَلُوْنَ خَبِيْرٌ ـ

45

ZA — زَ

Ending	Middle	Beginning
ـز	ـزـ	ز

English equivalent = z

Beginning:

زُ + رْ + تُ + مُ = زُرْتُمُ = حَتّٰى زُرْتُمُ الْمَقَابِرَ ۔
نُ + وِّ + جَ + تْ = نُوِّجَتْ = وَاِذَا النُّفُوْسُ زُوِّجَتْ ۔
نَ + سَ + جْ + ةٌ = نَجْرَةٌ = فَاِنَّمَا هِىَ زَجْرَةٌ وَّاحِدَةٌ ۔

Middle :

هُ + مَ + زَ + ةٍ = هُمَزَةٍ = وَيْلٌ لِّكُلِّ هُمَزَةٍ لُّمَزَةٍ ۔
بُ + رِّ + سَ + تْ = بُرِّزَتْ = وَبُرِّزَتِ الْجَحِيْمُ لِمَنْ يَّرٰى ۔
اُ + نْ + لِ + فَتْ = اُزْلِفَتْ = وَاِذَا الْجَنَّةُ اُزْلِفَتْ ۔

Ending:

عَ + زِ + ىْ + زٌ = عَزِيْزٌ = وَاللّٰهُ عَزِيْزٌ حَكِيْمٌ ۔
اَ + لْ + فَ + وْ + زُ = اَلْفَوْزُ = ذٰلِكَ الْفَوْزُ الْكَبِيْرُ ۔
اَ + لْ + سُّ + جْ + زَ = اَلرُّجْزَ = وَالرُّجْزَ فَاهْجُرْ ۔

46

س — SÎN

Ending	Middle	Beginning
ـس سـ	ـسـ	سـ

English equivalent = s

Beginning:

سَ + یَ + صْ + لْ + ی = سَیَصْلٰی نَارًا ذَاتَ لَهَبٍ ۔
سَ + نَ + سِ + مُ + هٗ = سَنَسِمُهٗ عَلَى الْخُرْطُوْمِ ۔
سِ + یٓ + ءَ + تْ = سِیْٓئَتْ وُجُوْهُ الَّذِیْنَ کَفَرُوْا ۔

Middle :

اَ + لْ + اِ + نْ + سَ + ا + نَ = اِلْاِنْسَانَ اِنَّ الْاِنْسَانَ لَفِیْ خُسْرٍ ۔
اَ + مْ + سَ + كَ = اَمْسَكَ اَمَّنْ هٰذَا الَّذِیْ یَرْزُقُکُمْ اِنْ اَمْسَکَ رِزْقَهٗ ۔
اَ + ل + سَّ + مْ + عَ = اَلسَّمْعَ اَلسَّمْعَ وَالْاَبْصَارَ وَالْاَفْئِدَةَ

Ending :

اَ + لَ + یْ + سَ = اَلَیْسَ اَلَیْسَ اللّٰهُ بِاَحْکَمِ الْحَاکِمِیْنَ ۔
بِ + ءْ + سَ = بِئْسَ وَبِئْسَ الْمَصِیْرُ ۔
لَ + یْ + سَ = لَیْسَ لَیْسَ لِوَقْعَتِهَا کَاذِبَةٌ ۔

47

ش – SHÎN

Ending	Middle	Beginning
ش ـش	ـشـ	شـ

English equivalent = sh

Beginning:

مِنْ شَرِّ مَا خَلَقَ ۔ =	شَرِّ =	شَ + رِّ
وَفِى الْاٰخِرَةِ عَذَابٌ شَدِيْدٌ ۔ = شَدِيْدٌ	حُ =	شَ + دِ + يْ +
فَشٰرِبُوْنَ شُرْبَ الْهِيْمِ ۔ =	شُرْبَ =	شَ + رُ + بَ

Middle:

رِحْلَةَ الشِّتَآءِ وَالصَّيْفِ ۔ = اَلشِّتَآءِ =	ء + ا + تَ + شِ + ل + اَ
فَهُوَ فِىْ عِيْشَةٍ رَّاضِيَةٍ ۔ = عِيْشَةٍ =	ةٍ + شَ + ىْ + عِ
اَلشَّمْسُ وَالْقَمَرُ بِحُسْبَانٍ = اَلشَّمْسُ =	سُ + مْ + شَّ + ل + اَ

Ending:

اَلْفَوَاحِشَ إِلَّا اللَّمَمَ ۔ = اَلْفَوَاحِشَ =	شَ + ا + حِ + وَ + فَ + لْ + اَ
اِلٰا يِلَافِ قُرَيْشٍ = قُرَيْشٍ =	شٍ + ىْ + رَ + قُ
عَرْشُ رَبِّكَ فَوْقَهُمْ يَوْمَئِذٍ ثَمٰنِيَةٌ ۔ = عَرْشُ =	شُ + رْ + عَ

ص – SÂD

Ending	Middle	Beginning
صى	ـصـ	صـ

English equivalent = s

Beginning:

صِ + رَ + ا + طَ = صِرَاطَ = صِرَاطَ الَّذِيْنَ اَنْعَمْتَ عَلَيْهِمْ
صٰ + دِ + قٖ + ىْ + نَ = صٰدِقٖيْنَ = اِنْ كَانُوْا صٰدِقٖيْنَ ۔
صَ + فًّ + ا = صَفًّا = اِنَّ اللهَ يُحِبُّ الَّذِيْنَ يُقَاتِلُوْنَ فِىْ سَبِيْلِهٖ صَفًّا

Middle:

سَ + ىَ + صْ + لٰى = سَيَصْلٰى = سَيَصْلٰى نَارًا ذَاتَ لَهَبٍ ۔
اَ + لْ + بَ + صَ + رُ = اَلْبَصَرُ = مَا زَاغَ الْبَصَرُ وَمَا طَغٰى ۔
مَ + صْ + فُ + وْ + نَ + ةٍ = مَصْفُوْنَةٍ = مُتَّكِبِيْنَ عَلٰى سُرُرٍ مَّصْفُوْنَةٍ ۔

Ending:

مَ + حِ + ىْ + صٍ = مَحِيْصٍ = مَالَهُمْ مِّنْ مَّحِيْصٍ ۔
مَ + رْ + صُ + وْ + صٌّ = مَرْصُوْصٌّ = كَاَنَّهُمْ بُنْيَانٌ مَّرْصُوْصٌّ ۔
نَ + قُ + صُّ = نَقُصُّ = كَذٰلِكَ نَقُصُّ عَلَيْكَ مِنْ اَنْبَاءِ مَا قَدْ سَبَقَ ۔

ض — DHÂD

Ending	Middle	Beginning
ـض	ـضـ	ضـ

English equivalent=dh

Beginning:

ضَ + رَ + بَ = ضَرَبَ = ضَرَبَ لَكُمْ مَثَلًا مِّنْ أَنْفُسِكُمْ۔
ضَ + رِيْ + عٍ = ضَرِيْعٍ = لَيْسَ لَهُمْ طَعَامٌ إِلَّا مِنْ ضَرِيْعٍ
ضَ + لَّ = ضَلَّ = مَا ضَلَّ صَاحِبُكُمْ وَمَا غَوَىٰ۔

Middle:

يَ + ضْ + رِ + بُ = يَضْرِبُ = وَيَضْرِبُ اللّٰهُ الْأَمْثَالَ لِلنَّاسِ۔
رَ + ا + ضِ + يَ + ةٌ = رَاضِيَةٌ = لِسَعْيِهَا رَاضِيَةٌ۔
مَ + وْ + ضُ + عَ + ةٌ = مَوْضُوعَةٌ = وَّالْأَكْوَابُ مَوْضُوعَةٌ۔

Ending:

يَ + حُ + ضُّ = يَحُضُّ = وَلَا يَحُضُّ عَلَىٰ طَعَامِ الْمِسْكِيْنِ۔
يَ + قْ + ضِ = يَقْضِ = كَلَّا لَمَّا يَقْضِ مَآ أَمَرَهُ۔
أَ + لْ + أَ + رْ + ضِ = الْأَرْضِ = وَفِي الْأَرْضِ آيٰتٌ لِّلْمُوْقِنِيْنَ۔

TÂ — ط

Ending	Middle	Beginning
ـط سط	ـطـ ـط	ط

English equivalent = ṭ

Beginning:

ط + ى + رُ + ا = طَيْرًا = وَأَرْسَلَ عَلَيْهِمْ طَيْرًا أَبَابِيلَ ۔
ط + غَ + وْ = طَغَوْ = اَلَّذِينَ طَغَوْا فِى الْبِلَادِ ۔
ط + عَ + ا + م = طَعَام = وَلَا تَحَاضُّونَ عَلَى طَعَامِ الْمِسْكِينِ ۔

Middle :

اَ + لْ + حَ + طَ + ب = اَلْحَطَبِ = وَامْرَأَتُهُ حَمَّالَةَ الْحَطَبِ ۔
مَ + طْ + لَ + ع = مَطْلَعِ = هِىَ حَتَّى مَطْلَعِ الْفَجْرِ ۔
سُ + طِ + حَ + تْ = سُطِحَتْ = وَإِلَى الْأَرْضِ كَيْفَ سُطِحَتْ ۔

Ending :

مُ + ج + ى + طٌ = مُحِيطٌ = وَاللهُ مُحِيطٌ بِالْكَافِرِينَ ۔
سَ + وْ + طَ = سَوْطَ = فَصَبَّ عَلَيْهِمْ رَبُّكَ سَوْطَ عَذَابٍ ۔
صِ + رَ + ا + طِ = صِرَاطِ = إِلَى سَوَاءِ الصِّرَاطِ ۔

ZÂ – ظ

Ending	Middle	Beginning
ـظ	ـظـ	ظـ

English equivalent = ẓ

Beginning:

ظَ + هـ + رَ + كَ = ظَهَرَكَ - اَلَّذِىْ اَنْقَضَ ظَهْرَكَ ۔
ظَ + هـ + رَ = ظَهَرَ = ظَهَرَ الْفَسَادُ فِى الْبَرِّ وَالْبَحْرِ ۔
ظُ + لـ + مِ + هِـ + مْ = ظُلْمِهِمْ = وَاِنَّ رَبَّكَ لَذُوْ مَغْفِرَةٍ لِّلنَّاسِ عَلٰى ظُلْمِهِمْ ۔

Middle :

اَ + لـ + ظّ + نّ = اَلظَّنِّ = اِنَّ بَعْضَ الظَّنِّ اِثْمٌ ۔
اَ + ظـ + لَ + مُ = اَظْلَمُ = مَنْ اَظْلَمُ مِمَّنْ كَتَمَ شَهَادَةً ۔
حـ + فِ + ظـ + وْ + نَ = حٰفِظُوْنَ = اِنَّا نَحْنُ نَزَّلْنَا الذِّكْرَ وَاِنَّا لَهٗ لَحٰفِظُوْنَ

Ending :

حَ + فِ + يْ + ظُ = حَفِيْظٌ = اِنَّ رَبِّىْ عَلٰى كُلِّ شَىْءٍ حَفِيْظٌ ۔
غَ + لِ + يْ + ظُ = غَلِيْظٌ = وَمِنْ وَّرَآئِهٖ عَذَابٌ غَلِيْظٌ
حَ + فِ + يْ + ظُ = حَفِيْظٌ = اِنِّىْ حَفِيْظٌ عَلِيْمٌ ۔

‘AIN — ع

Ending	Middle	Beginning
ع ع	عـ ـعـ	عـ

English equivalent-‘a

Beginning:

عَ + ا + بِ + دُ = عَابِدٌ = وَلَا أَنَا عَابِدٌ مَّا عَبَدْتُّمْ ۔			
عَ + دَّ + ةُ = عَدَّدَهُ = ٱلَّذِى جَمَعَ مَالًا وَّعَدَّدَةُ ۔			
عَ + لَّ + مَ = عَلَّمَ = عَلَّمَ الْإِنْسَانَ مَالَمْ يَعْلَمْ ۔			

Middle :

نَ + عُ + بُ + دُ = نَعْبُدُ = إِيَّاكَ نَعْبُدُ وَإِيَّاكَ نَسْتَعِينْ ۔			
اَ + لْ + عَ + صْ + رِ = الْعَصْرِ = وَالْعَصْرِ ۔			
تَ + عْ + لَ + مُ + وْ + نَ = تَعْلَمُوْنَ = كَلَّا سَوْفَ تَعْلَمُوْنَ ۔			

Ending :

تَ + طْ + لِ + عُ = تَطَّلِعُ = ٱلَّتِى تَطَّلِعُ عَلَى الْأَفْئِدَةِ ۔			
مَ + طْ + لَ + عِ = مَطْلَعِ = هِىَ حَتَّى مَطْلَعِ الْفَجْرِ ۔			
مَ + عَ = مَعَ = فَإِنَّ مَعَ الْعُسْرِ يُسْرًا ۔			

GHAIN – غ

Ending	Middle	Beginning
غ	غـ	غـ

English equivalent = gh

Beginning:

غَ + يْ + رِ = غَيْرِ = غَيْرِ الْمَغْضُوبِ عَلَيْهِمْ وَلَا الضَّآلِّيْنَ ۔

| غَ + رَّ + كَ = غَرَّكَ = يَـٰٓأَيُّهَا الْاِنْسَانُ مَا غَرَّكَ بِرَبِّكَ الْكَرِيْمِ ۔ |

| غَ + بَ + رَ + ةٌ = غَبَرَةٌ = وَوُجُوْهٌ يَّوْمَئِذٍ عَلَيْهَا غَبَرَةٌ ۔ |

Middle :

| اَلْغَفُوْرُ = اِنَّهٗ هُوَ الْغَفُوْرُ الرَّحِيْمُ ۔ = اٰ + لْ + غَ + فُ + وْ + رُ |

| مَسْغَبَةٍ = فِىْ يَوْمٍ ذِىْ مَسْغَبَةٍ ۔ = مَ + سْ + غَ + بَ + ةٍ |

| يَغْشٰى = اِذْ يَغْشَى السِّدْرَةَ مَا يَغْشٰى ۔ = يَ + غْ + شَ + ىٰ |

Ending :

| بَلَغَ = وَلَمَّا بَلَغَ اَشُدَّهٗ اٰتَيْنَاهُ حُكْمًا وَّعِلْمًا ۔ = بَ + لَ + غَ |

| زَاغَ = مَا زَاغَ الْبَصَرُ وَمَا طَغٰى ۔ = زَ + ا + غَ |

| نُفْرِغُ = سَنَفْرُغُ لَكُمْ اَيُّهَ الثَّقَلٰنِ ۔ = نُ + فْ + رُ + غُ |

54

ف – FÂ

Ending	Middle	Beginning
ن	ـفـ	ف

English equivalent = f

Beginning:

فِ + ی = فِی	اَلَّذِیْ یُوَسْوِسُ فِیْ صُدُوْرِ النَّاسِ ۔
فِ + نَ + عَ + وْ + نُ = فِرْعَوْنَ	فِرْعَوْنَ وَثَمُوْدَ ۔
فَ + بَ + شِّ + رُ + هُ + مْ = فَبَشِّرْهُمْ	فَبَشِّرْهُمْ بِعَذَابٍ اَلِیْمٍ ۔

Middle:

اَ + لْ + فَ + لَ + قِ = اَلْفَلَقِ	قُلْ اَعُوْذُ بِرَبِّ الْفَلَقِ ۔
نَ + فْ + سٌ = نَفْسٌ	یَوْمَ لَا تَمْلِكُ نَفْسٌ لِّنَفْسٍ شَیْئًا ۔
مُ + سْ + فِ + رَ + ۃٌ = مُسْفِرَۃٌ	وُجُوْهٌ یَّوْمَئِذٍ مُّسْفِرَۃٌ ۔

Ending:

اَ + لْ + صَّ + یْ + فِ = اَلصَّیْفِ	رِحْلَۃَ الشِّتَآءِ وَالصَّیْفِ ۔
صُ + حُ + فِ = صُحُفِ	صُحُفِ اِبْرَاهِیْمَ وَمُوْسَی ۔
کَ + یْ + فَ = کَیْفَ	اَفَلَا یَنْظُرُوْنَ اِلَی الْاِبِلِ کَیْفَ خُلِقَتْ ۔

ق — QÂF

Ending	Middle	Beginning
ﻖ	ـقـ	ﻗ

English equivalent=q

Beginning:

قُ + لْ = قُلْ = قُلْ اَعُوْذُ بِرَبِّ النَّاسِ ۔		
قُ + تِ + لَ = قُتِلَ = قُتِلَ اَصْحٰبُ الْاُخْدُوْدِ ۔		
قُ + عُ + وْ + دٌ = قُعُوْدٌ = اِذْ هُمْ عَلَيْهَا قُعُوْدٌ ۔		

Middle :

اَ + لْ + یَ + قِ + يْ + نِ = اَلْيَقِيْنِ = ثُمَّ لَتَرَوُنَّهَا عَيْنَ الْيَقِيْنِ ۔		
اَ + لْ + قَ + تْ = اَلْقَتْ = وَاَلْقَتْ مَا فِيْهَا وَ تَخَلَّتْ ۔		
مَ + رُ + قْ + وْ + مٌ = مَرْقُوْمٌ = كِتٰبٌ مَّرْقُوْمٌ ۔		

Ending :

اَ + لْ + فَ + لَ + قْ = اَلْفَلَقْ = قُلْ اَعُوْذُ بِرَبِّ الْفَلَقِ ۔		
وَ + سَ + قَ = وَسَقَ = وَالَّيْلِ وَمَا وَسَقَ ۔		
خَ + لَ + قَ = خَلَقَ = اَلَّذِىْ خَلَقَ فَسَوّٰى ۔		

ك — KÂF

Ending	Middle	Beginning
ـك ملك	ـك ـكـ	ك

English equivalent=k

Beginning:

ـكَ + سَ + بَ = كَسَبَ = مَاۤ اَغْنٰى عَنْهُ مَالُهُ وَمَاكَسَبَ ۔
ـكَ + فَ + رُ + وۡ + ا = كَفَرُوۡا = بَلِ الَّذِیۡنَ كَفَرُوۡا فِیۡ تَكۡذِیۡبٍ ۔
ـكَ + یۡ = كَیۡفَ = وَ اِلَى الۡاَرۡضِ كَیۡفَ سُطِحَتۡ ۔

Middle :

یَ + كُ + نۡ = یَكُنۡ = وَلَمۡ یَكُنۡ لَّهُ كُفُوًا اَحَدٌ ۔
سَ + بَ + كُ + مۡ = رَبُّكُمۡ = فَقَالَ اَنَا رَبُّكُمُ الۡاَعۡلٰى ۔
اَ + هۡ + لَ + كُ + تُ = اَهۡلَكۡتُ = یَقُوۡلُ اَهۡلَكۡتُ مَالًا لُّبَدًا ۔

Ending :

مَ + لِ + كِ = مٰلِكِ = مٰلِكِ یَوۡمِ الدِّیۡنِ ۔
مَ + سَ + كُ = مِسۡكُ = خِتٰمُهٗ مِسۡكٌ ۔
ذَا + لِ + كَ = ذٰلِكَ = وَفِیۡ ذٰلِكَ فَلۡیَتَنَافَسِ الۡمُتَنَافِسُوۡنَ ۔

LÂM — ل

Ending	Middle	Beginning
لـ مـل	ـلـ	ل

English equivalent=l

Beginning:

لَكُمْ دِيْنُكُمْ وَلِيَ دِيْنَ۔	=	لَكُمُ	=	م	+	كُ	+ لَ
لَمْ يَكُنِ الَّذِيْنَ كَفَرُوْا۔	=	لَمُ	=	مُ	+	لَ
لَتَرَوُنَّ الْجَحِيْمَ۔	= لَتَرَوُنَّ	نَّ	+	وُ	+	رَ	+	تَ	+ لَ

Middle :

وَلَا يَحُضُّ عَلَى طَعَامِ الْمِسْكِيْنِ۔	= عَلَى	=	ى	+	لَ	+ عَ
الَّتِيْ تَطَّلِعُ عَلَى الْاَفْئِدَةِ۔	= تَطَّلِعُ	عُ	+	لِ	+	طَّ	+ تَ
هِيَ حَتّى مَطْلَعِ الْفَجْرِ۔	= مَطْلَع	عِ	+	لَ	+	طْ	+ مَ

Ending :

وَيْلٌ لِكُلِّ هُمَزَةٍ لُّمَزَةٍ۔	=	وَيْلٌ	=	لٌ	+	ىْ	+ وَ
وَاَنْتَ حِلٌّ بِهذَا الْبَلَدِ۔	=	حِلٌّ	=	لٌّ	+ جِ
اَلَمْ نَجْعَلْ لَّهُ عَيْنَيْنِ۔	= نَجْعَلُ	لُ	+	عَ	+	جْ	+ نَ

مـ — MÎM

Ending	Middle	Beginning
مـ	ـمـ	مـ

English equivalent=m

Beginning:

مَ + لِ + كِ = مَلِكِ = مَلِكِ النَّاسِ ۔
مَ + سْ + غَ + بَ + ةٍ = مَسْغَبَةٍ = اَوْ اِطْعَمٌ فِيْ يَوْمٍ ذِيْ مَسْغَبَةٍ ۔
مَ + رْ + قُ + وْ + مٌ = مَرْقُوْمٌ = كِتَابٌ مَّرْقُوْمٌ ۔

Middle:

اَ + لْ + حَ + مْ + دُ = اَلْحَمْدُ = اَلْحَمْدُ لِلّٰهِ رَبِّ الْعٰلَمِيْنَ ۔
ثَ + مُ + وْ + دُ = ثَمُوْدُ = وَثَمُوْدَ الَّذِيْنَ جَابُوا الصَّخْرَ بِالْوَادِ
تَ + مْ + لِ + كُ = تَمْلِكُ = يَوْمَ لَا تَمْلِكُ نَفْسٌ لِّنَفْسٍ شَيْئًا

Ending:

اَ + لْ + رَّ + حِ + يْ + مِ = الرَّحِيْمِ = الرَّحْمٰنِ الرَّحِيْمِ ۔
اَ + لِ + يْ + مِ = اَلِيمٍ = فَبَشِّرْهُمْ بِعَذَابٍ اَلِيمٍ ۔
اَ + لْ + نَّ + عِ + يْ + مِ = النَّعِيْمِ = ثُمَّ لَتُسْئَلُنَّ يَوْمَئِذٍ عَنِ النَّعِيْمِ ۔

NÛN – ن

Ending	Middle	Beginning
ن	ـنـ	نـ

English equivalent = n

Beginning:

اِذَا جَآءَ نَصْرُ اللّٰهِ وَالْفَتْحُ ۔	=	نَصُرُ =	رُ + صُ + نَ
اَلَمْ نَشْرَحْ لَكَ صَدْرَكَ ۔	=	نَشْرَحْ =	حْ + رَ + شْ + نَ
وَنَفْسٍ وَّمَا سَوَّاهَا ۔	=	نَفْسٍ =	سٍ + فْ + نَ

Middle:

وَرَاَيْتَ النَّاسَ ۔	=	اَلنَّاسَ =	سَ + ا + نَّ + ل + اَ
اِنَّ الْاِنْسَانَ لِرَبِّهٖ لَكَنُوْدٌ ۔	=	لَكَنُوْدٌ =	دٌ + و + نُ + كَ + لَ
فَاِنَّ الْجَنَّةَ هِىَ الْمَاْوٰى ۔	=	اَلْجَنَّةَ =	ةَ + نَّ + جَ + ل + اَ

Ending:

يَدْخُلُوْنَ فِىْ دِيْنِ اللّٰهِ اَفْوَاجًا ۔	=	دِيْنِ =	نِ + ىْ + دِ
يَخْرُجُ مِنْۢ بَيْنِ الصُّلْبِ وَالتَّرَآئِبِ ۔	=	بَيْنِ =	نِ + ىْ + بَ
اِنَّهٗ ظَنَّ اَنْ لَّنْ يَّحُوْرَ ۔	=	ظَنَّ =	نَّ + ظَ

HÂ — هـ

Ending	Middle	Beginning
ـه	ـهـ	هـ

English equivalent=h

Beginning:

هُ + مُ + زَ + ةٍ = هُمَزَةٍ = وَيْلٌ لِّكُلِّ هُمَزَةٍ لُّمَزَةٍ

هَ + دَ + يْ + نٰهُ = هَدَيْنٰهُ = وَهَدَيْنٰهُ النَّجْدَيْنِ ۔

هَ + لْ = هَلْ = هَلْ اَتٰىكَ حَدِيْثُ الْغَاشِيَةِ ۔

Middle :

اَ + لْ + هٰ + كُ + مُ = اَلْهٰكُمُ = اَلْهٰكُمُ التَّكَاثُرُ ۔

ظَ + هٰ + رَ + كَ = ظَهْرَكَ = اَلَّذِىْ اَنْقَضَ ظَهْرَكَ ۔

تَ + قْ + هَ + رْ = تَقْهَرْ = فَاَمَّا الْيَتِيْمَ فَلَا تَقْهَرْ ۔

Ending :

اَ + لْ + لَ + ا + هُ = اَللهُ = قُلْ هُوَ اللهُ اَحَدٌ ۔

خِ + تٰ + مُ + هٗ = خِتٰمُهٗ = خِتٰمُهٗ مِسْكٌ ۔

اَ + هْ + لِ + هٖ = اَهْلِهٖ = اِنَّهٗ كَانَ فِىْٓ اَهْلِهٖ مَسْرُوْرًا ۔

و — WAW

Ending	Middle	Beginning
و	و	و

English equivalent = w

Beginning:

وَ + قَ + بَ = وَقَبَ	= وَمِنْ شَرِّ غَاسِقٍ إِذَا وَقَبَ -
وِ + نْ + رَ + كَ = وِزْرَكَ	= وَوَضَعْنَا عَنْكَ وِزْرَكَ
وَ + سَ + قَ = وَسَقَ	= وَالَّيْلِ وَمَا وَسَقَ -

Middle :

تَ + وَ + ا + صَ + وْ + ا = تَوَاصَوْا = وَتَوَاصَوْا بِالصَّبْرِ -
ىَ + دُ + عُ + وْ + ا = يَدْعُوا = فَسَوْفَ يَدْعُوا ثُبُورًا ۟ ـ
لَ + قَ + وْ + لُ = لَقَوْلُ = إِنَّهُ لَقَوْلُ فَصْلٌ ۟ ـ

Ending :

هُ + وَ = هُوَ = إِنَّ شَانِئَكَ هُوَ الْأَبْتَرُ -
رَ + ضُ + وْ + ا = رَضُوا = رَضِيَ اللّٰهُ عَنْهُمْ وَرَضُوا عَنْهُ ۟
فَ + هُ + وَ = فَهُوَ = فَهُوَ فِي عِيشَةٍ رَّاضِيَةٍ -

YÂ – ى

Ending	Middle	Beginning
ى	يـ	بـ
	English equivalent=y	

Beginning:

لَمْ يَلِدْ وَلَمْ يُوْلَدْ ۔ =	يَلِدْ =	دْ +	لِ +	ىَ
وَيَنْقَلِبُ اِلٰٓى اَهْلِهٖ مَسْرُوْرًا ۔ = يَنْقَلِبُ =	قَ + لِ + نْ + ىَ			ب +
اِنَّهٗ هُوَ يُبْدِئُ وَيُعِيْدُ ۔ = يُبْدِئُ =	ئُ +	دِ +	بْ +	ىُ

Middle :

فِىْ جِيْدِهَا حَبْلٌ مِّنْ مَّسَدٍ ۔ = جِيْدِهَا =	ا + هَ + دِ + ىْ + جِ			
وَاللّٰهُ مِنْ وَّرَآئِهِمْ مُّحِيْطٌ ۔ = مُحِيْطٌ =	طٌ +	ىْ +	حِ +	مُ
وَاَكِيْدُ كَيْدًا ۔ = اَكِيْدُ =	دُ +	ىْ +	كِ +	اَ

Ending :

اِنَّ الْاِنْسَانَ لَفِىْ خُسْرٍ ۔ = لَفِىْ =	ى +	فِ +	لَ
ثُمَّ لَا يَمُوْتُ فِيْهَا وَلَا يَحْيٰى ۔ = يَحْيٰى =	ىٰ +	حْ +	ىَ
لَكُمْ دِيْنُكُمْ وَلِىَ دِيْنِ ۔ =	لِىَ = ىَ + لِ

HAMZA — ء

Ending	Middle	Beginning
ء	مئ	ا

English equivalent=none

Beginning:

أَ + رَ + ءَ + ئَ + تَ = اَرَءَيْتَ = اَرَءَيْتَ الَّذِىْ يُكَذِّبُ بِالدِّيْنِ ۔

أَ + نِ + فَ + تِ = اَنِفَتِ = اَنِفَتِ الْاَرْضَ فَـةٌ ۔

أَ + فَ + سَ + ءَ + ئَ + تَ = اَفَرَءَيْتَ = اَفَرَءَيْتَ الَّذِىْ تَوَلَّى ۔

Middle :

شَ + ا + نِ + ئُ + كَ = شَانِئُكَ = اِنَّ شَانِئَكَ هُوَ الْاَبْتَرُ ۔

بِ + ءُ + سَ = بِئْسَ = وَبِئْسَ الْمَصِيْرُ ۔

ىَ + سُ + ءَ + لُ = يَسْئَلُ = يَسْئَلُ اَيَّانَ يَوْمُ الْقِيَامَةِ ۔

Ending :

جَ + آ + ءَ = جَآءَ = اِذَا جَآءَ نَصْرُ اللهِ وَالْفَتْحُ ۔

اَ + ل + سَّ + مَ + آ + ءِ = اَلسَّمَآءِ = وَالسَّمَآءِ وَالطَّارِقِ ۔

شَ + آ + ءَ = شَآءَ = فِىْ اَيِّ صُوْرَةٍ مَّا شَآءَ رَكَّبَكَ ۔

Ta Marbutah — ة
Ta-al-Tanîth

Ending	Ending
تـة	ة

English equivalent=t

This letter occurs only at the end of a word.

Beginning:

اَ + لْ + مُ + وْ + قَ + دَ + ةِ = اَلْمُوْقَدَةِ = نَارُ اللّٰهِ الْمُوْقَدَةِ ۚ

اَ + لْ + مَ + غْ + فِ + رَ + ةِ = اَلْمَغْفِرَةِ = هُوَ اَهْلُ التَّقْوٰى وَاَهْلُ الْمَغْفِرَةِ ۗ

قَ + سْ + وَ + رَ + ةٍ = قَسْوَرَةٍ = فَرَّتْ مِنْ قَسْوَرَةٍ ۚ

Ending:

حَ + مَّ + ا + لَ + ةَ = حَمَّالَةَ = حَمَّالَةَ الْحَطَبِ ۚ

فَ + ا + كِ + هَ + ةٍ = فَاكِهَةٍ = وَفَاكِهَةٍ كَثِيْرَةٍ ۚ

ثُ + لَّ + ةٌ = ثُلَّةٌ = وَثُلَّةٌ مِّنَ الْاٰخِرِيْنَ ۚ

65

SILENT LETTERS
Sukûn followed by Shaddah

Whenever a letter with Sukûn is followed by a letter with Shaddah, the letter with Sukûn becomes silent. **It will not be** pronounced.

Separately Pronounced: تَأْتِيهِمْ   كَانَتْ   مِنْ مَآءٍ

But while connecting them: كَانَتَّأْتِيهِمْ   مِمَّآءٍ

Separately Pronounced: قُلْ لِمَنْ   مَا   مِنْ مَسَدٍ

But while connecting them: قُلْ لِمَنْ مَّا   مِمَّسَدٍ

Same thing happens in the following words:

عَقَّدْتُمْ   نَخْلُقُكُمْ   عَبَدْتُمْ

SILENT LETTERS
Followed by رّ and لّ

Some letters become completely silent, for example if after a نْ (Nûn with Sukûn), رّ or لّ follows, the نْ becomes completely silent, letting earlier letter in the word connect with the following رّ or لّ in pronunciation.

Letter نْ Nûn with Sukûn becoming silent while connecting two words

مِنْ رَّبِّهِمْ

ر

- نْ is not pronounced
- مْ of the first word is directly connecting with رّ of the second word
- A Shaddah appears in the merging letter

يَكُنْ لَّمْ

ل

- نْ is not pronounced
- كُ in first word is directly connected to لّ of the second word.
- A Shaddah appears in the merging letter لّ

SILENT LETTERS
Nunation followed by ل & ر

If a ر or ل follows a Nunation ـٌـٍـً , the sound of Nunation completely disappears. Instead of ـٌـٍـً a vowel of ـُـِـَ is pronounced while connecting the first word to the next word. It means that ـٌ becomes ـُ , ـٍ becomes ـِ and ـً becomes ـَ if it is followed by ر or ل

ر = أُمَّةٍ رَّسُوْلاً   غَفُوْرًا رَّحِيْمًا   غَفُوْرٌ رَّحِيْمٌ

ل = خَيْرٌ لِّلَّذِيْنَ   اشْتَانًا لِّيَرَوْا   يَوْمَئِذٍ لَّخَبِيْرٌ

SILENT LETTERS
نْ Followed by ن , م , و or ى

If a نْ (Nûn with Sukûn) is at the end of a word and either ن , م , و or ى is the first letter in the next word, the letter نْ (Nûn with Sukûn) becomes partially silent, leaving a low nasal sound, called Ghunnah.

Examples	
مَنْ يَّقُوْلُ	مَنْ يَّشَآءُ
مِنْ وَّلِيٍّ	مِنْ مِّثْلِهٖ
مِنْ نُّطْفَةٍ	أَنْ نَّقُوْلَ

SILENT LETTERS
Nunation followed by ن , م , و or ى

If a Tanween ـًـٍـٌ (Nunation) is at the end of a word and either ن , م , و or ى is the first letter in the next word, the sound of nunation will partially disappear while reading both words together. A slight nasal sound, called Ghunnah will show in pronunciation of both words when combined.

ى =	كُلٌّ يَّجْرِيْ	سَبِيْلاً يَّوَيُدَتِى	لِقَوْمٍ يُّؤْمِنُوْنَ
و =	مَغْفِرَةٌ وَّاَجْرٌ	قِيَامًا وَّقُعُوْدًا	لَهَبٍ وَّتَبَّ
م =	ذُرِّيَّةً مِّنْ	ثَوَابًا مِّنْ	بِسُوْرَةٍ مِّنْ
ن =	حِطَّةٌ نَّغْفِرْ	جَالاً نُّوْحِى	شَىْءٌ نَّحْنُ

〰〰〰〰〰〰〰〰

SILENT أ (Hamzat-al-Wasl)

Hamza is usually seen with Alif (أ إ آ) Hamzat-at-Wasl (the joining hamza) is not pronounced during a continued reading. This hamza written as ص at the top of an ا means that Alif beneath it should not be pronounced.

Examples	
وَاٱمْرَاَتُهٗ	هٰذَاٱلْبَيْتِ
اَللهُ ٱلصَّمَدُ	وَٱنْحَرْ
هُوَٱلْاَبْتَرُ	رِحْلَةَ ٱلشِّتَآءِ

The Arabic letters are divided into two groups:(1) Shamsi letters and (2) Qamari letters.

If for particularization an Alif and Lâm ا ل are prefixed to any one of the Shamsi letters, the letter Lâm ل is not pronounced.

There are 14 Shamsi letters:

اَلـدِّيْنَ	د	اَلتَّكَاثُرُ	ت	اَلسَّاجِدِيْنَ	س
اَلـذَّاكِرِيْنَ	ذ	اَلثُّلُثِ	ث	اَلشِّتَآءَ	ش
اَلرَّحْمٰنِ	ر	اَلصَّمَدُ	ص	اَلطَّيِّبُ	ط
اَلـزَّكَوٰةِ	ز	اَلضَّآلِّيْنَ	ض	اَلظَّنِّ	ظ
اَللَّيْلِ	ل			اَلنَّاسِ	ن

WHEN ل IS PRONOUNCED

If ال are prefixed to any one of the Qamari letters, the letter ل is pronounced clearly. For example in اَلْقَمَرُ the letter ل is pronounced.

There are 13 Qamari letters:

اَلْفَلَقِ	ف	اَلْجِنَّةِ	ج	الْاِنْسَانَ	أ
اَلْقَارِعَةُ	ق	اَلْخَطِيْبُ	ح	اَلْبَلَاغُ	ب
اَلْكَافِرُوْنَ	ك	اَلْخَنَّاسِ	خ	اَلْعٰلَمِيْنَ	ع
اَلْوَسْوَاسِ	و	اَلْمِسْكِيْنِ	م	اَلْغَيْبِ	غ
		اَلْيَتِيْمَ	ى		

While reading in continuation with a word before it, ا of ال is skipped to connect a Qamari letter.

Therefore:

حَمَّالَةَ الْحَطَبِ	←	حَمَّالَةَ اَلْحَطَبِ
رَبِّ الْفَلَقِ	←	رَبِّ اَلْفَلَقِ

WHEN ال ARE NOT PRONOUNCED

When reading in continuation with a word that begins with ال, both ال are skipped to connect to the Shamsi letter. The reason is that ا is Hamzat-al-Wasl and ل is occuring before a Shamsi letter.

Therefore:

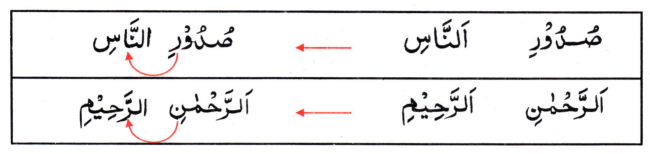

SUBSTITUTING WITH ن

If after a letter with Nunation ‐ a Hamzat-al-Wasl ا comes, the following will happen in reading it.

1) The letter with Nunation will retain only one vowel. For Example:

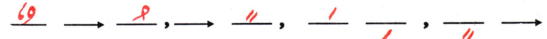

2) A small Nûn with Kasrah ن appears below ا
3) The last letter of the first word will be connected with the following word with ن sound.

نُوْحُ اِبْنَهٗ	←
شَيْئًا اِتَّخَذَ	←

This is the reason when قُلْ هُوَ اللّٰهُ أَحَدٌ is read in continuity with, اللّٰهُ الصَّمَدُ it is read as;

أَحَدُنِ اللّٰهُ الصَّمَدُ

SUBSTITUTING WITH م

If the letter ب comes after نْ (Nûn with Sukûn) or Nunation ـٌ ـً ـٍ, the نْ or Nunation sound is substituted as follows:

1) ـٌ sound will change to ـُ sound
   ـً sound will change to ـَ sound
   ـٍ sound will change to ـِ sound
2) If it is a نْ it will be disregarded
3) A small م will show up before
4) A nasal م sound will be pronounced

For Example:	
مُسْتَخْفٍۢ بِالَّيْلِ	عَلِيمٌۢ بِذَاتِ
مِنۢ بَعْدِهٖ	خَبِيرًۢا بَصِيرًا

Note: If the letter ب comes after نْ even within a word, the نْ sound is substituted with a nasal م sound.

أَنۢبِيَآءُ	يَنۢبُوعًا

Qur'ân printed in Arab countries disregards Tanween in this situation: عَلِيمٌ بِذَاتِ

STOP CAUSES VOWEL CHANGE

at the Last Letter

If a Qur'ân reader makes a stop at any word, the person must invariably pronounce the last letter of that word with Sukûn.

This rule will apply regardless of any symbol on the last letter.

اَلنَّاسْ Will be pronounced	اَلنَّاسُ if you stop there.
خَلَقْ Will be pronounced	خَلَقُ if you stop there.
أُحَـدْ Will be pronounced	أُحَـدٌ if you stop there.
لَهَبْ Will be pronounced	لَهَبٍ if you stop there.

Exception: If stopping at a word ending with a Fathah Nunation ___⁄⁄___ , one must stop with a short Maddah ___ا___ instead of ___ً___ Nunation.

نِسَآءَا Will be pronounced	نِسَآءً if you stop there.
عَمَّى Will be pronounced	عَمًى if you stop there.

STOP CAUSES  TO SOUND LIKE

If you stop reading where there is a round Ta ة , it is pronounced like a Ha ه with Sukûn, no matter what vowel it has.

اَلْجَنَّهْ Will be pronounced	اَلْجَنَّةُ if you stop there.
اَلْحَرَكَهْ Will be pronounced	اَلْحَرَكَةُ if you stop there.
لُمَزَهْ Will be pronounced	لُمَزَةٍ if you stop there.
اَلْحُطَمَةْ Will be pronounced	اَلْحُطَمَهُ if you stop there.
اَلْمُوْقَدَةْ Will be pronounced	اَلْمُوْقَدَةُ if you stop there.

Note: If there is a long Tâ ت at the end of a word where you stop reading, it does not become Ha ه . It remains a ت but is pronounced with a Sukûn.

اَلْبَيْتْ Will be pronounced	اَلْبَيْتُ if you stop.
جَنَّتْ Will be pronounced	جَنَّتُ if you stop.

Note: If a stop is made over a letter with Shaddah ــّـ at the end of a word, vowel will change to Sukûn, but the letter must be pronounced with emphasis in order to distinguish between ــّـ and a ــّـ Example: تَبَّ

مَخَارِجُ الْحُرُوفِ
SEE TAJWEED RULES

Figure 1:

وَرَتِّلِ الْقُرْءَانَ تَرْتِيلًا

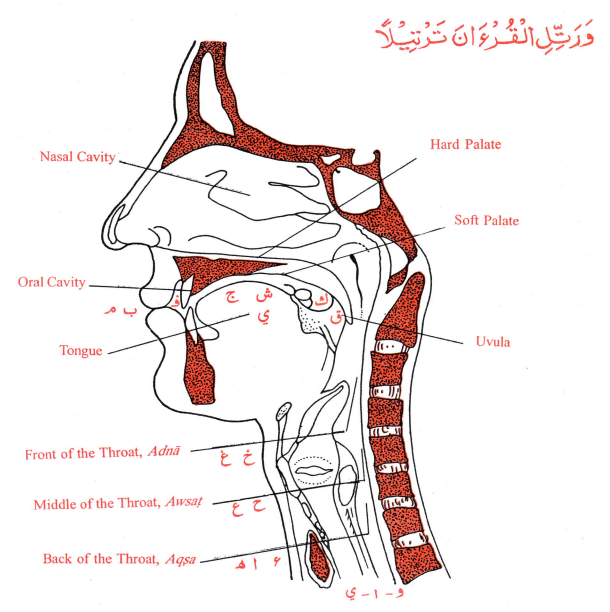

Figure 1: Cross Section Showing the Nose, Mouth and Throat

TAJWEED RULES

(See Figure - 1) pg. 75

Makhârij مَخَارِجُ الْحُرُوف (Points of Articulation)

The point of articulation (i.e., The place of pronunciation) of a letter in Arabic alphabet is called its *Makhraj* (مَخْرَج plural, *Makhârij* مَخَارِج). They are derived from the root word خَرَجَ (*Kharaja*) which means to emit, exit, emerge.

In order to feel the *makhraj* of a letter (حُرُوف), add a hamzah fatha (أَ , أَ) before the letter and make the letter Sâkin (سَاكِن , e.g., ب) and then pronounce the letter. For example, Hamzah Fatha Bâ *sâkin* (أَب)= 'Ab; Hamzah Fatha Lam Sâkin (أَلْ)= 'Al, etc. For practice, see more examples in Table 1 (p.8):

Remember that whenever there is a *harakah* (ُ , ِ , َ , a short vowel sign) over ا (Alif), e.g., أ - إ - أ), then the alif becomes a hamzah, like (أُ إِ أَ), so it is no longer an alif. In certain prints of *Mus.haf* (i.e., the Qur'ân in Arabic), it is marked with a *sukûn* (°) on top of it like. In some prints, a small *hamzah* with a *sukûn* is actually put on it, for example, *Ma'kul* مَأْكُول

If there is no *harakah* or *sukûn* over *Alif* (for example, in Mâ ما Lâ لا), it is then simply an *Alif*, and the preceding fatha harakah is prolonged – normally two times long (as a natural madd or prolongation that will be discussed later).

Alif is also written in the form of a shortened *Alif* as a long vowel sign above a letter and it is called *alif maqsurah* (مَقْصُورَة) or Fatha Tawilah. For instance, هٰذَا (Hâdhâ) has a shortened alif over the letter ه (Hâ) and an alif in its regular form after that letter ذ (Dhâl). The duration of prolongation of both is the same– two measures of a *harakah* (short vowels), or a standard measure of one alif.

It should be remembered that Alif (ا) is never the first letter in a word, it always comes after another letter. More often, a hamzah comes as the first letter in a word. The word أَذَان ('Azân) has both hamzah and alif. The first letter (ا) before the letter Dhâl (ذ) is a *hamzah* because it has a *harakah*, and the one after <u>Dhâl</u> (ذ) is alif(ا) because it does not have any *harakah*.

N.B. Learn the proper use of the makhârij (مَخَارِجْ) from a learned Qâri and practise them until you fully master them. Then the recitation of the Qur'ân with proper tajweed will become easy. Tape recorded voices for *Makhârij* and pronunciations will be helpful for practising correct recitation to some extent.

There are twenty nine (29) letters in the Arabic alphabet:

ا ب ت ث ج ح خ د ذ ر ز س ش ص ض

ط ظ ع غ ف ق ك ل م ن ه و ء ى

A distinction should be made between the two words: 'letters' and 'sound'. Letters are written symbols representing elements of the alphabet, while sounds are the possible ways of pronuncing those letter symbols. Unlike the letters of the English alphabet, each Arabic letter normally has only one sound. Notice the different sound of u in English words: but and put, and the sound of a in car, care and man, etc. In the words: city, busy, women and pretty, the letters I, u, o, e stand for one and same (e) sound. In Arabic we do not find such variations.

Speech sounds are conveniently classified on an articulatory basis into vowels and consonants. A vowel is defined as a voiced sound produced by a continuous stream of air, which passes through the pharynx and mouth without any obstruction. In Qur'ânic recitation, vowels can be either short, which are represented by the signs ___ , ___ , ___ or long represented by the letters ا , ى , و or preceded by ___ , ___ or ___ respectively. e.g., بُو رِي بَا

Consonants are the sounds whose articulation is accompanied by some closure or narrowing in the speech tract; thus, the escape of air is momentarily prevented or associated with some audible friction. The letters و and ى may also behave as 'semivowels'. Consonants can be classified according to the manner of their articulation.

According to the agreed upon view of the majority of the scholars, grammarians, phoneticians and Qâries , there are in all seventeen (17) *Makhârij* – places from which Arabic Letters emanate. They are listed in order (from innermost to outermost) below, showing the letters which come out from each *makhraj*, under different areas of speech (A – F):

A. Al-Jawf اَلْجَوْفْ (the interior or chest area):

1. حُرُوفُ الْمَدّ Maddah Letters

The interior is one makhraj in itself and includes the empty area of the open mouth. From it emerge

The Vowel sounds of *maddah* letters و (waw), ى (Yâ) and ا (Alif), provided that و (waw) is sakin and the preceding letter bears a *Dhammah* (ُو), for example, تُو , خُوَا ; ى is *sakin* and the preceding letter has a *Kasrah*, for example, تِى , رِى ; and (alif) which by definition is always sâkin, and the preceding letter has a *fathah*, for example رَا , حَا . All these three maddah letters are found in the mnemonic word تُوحِيْهَا

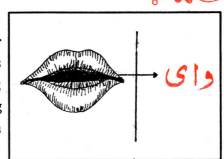

B.   Guttural (Throat) Letters (6)   حُرُوفُ الْحَلْقِ

2.   Aqsa al-Halq – (2): أَقْصَى الْحَلْقِ

The deepest (back) part of the throat is the *makhraj* of *Hamzah* (ء). It is a true written consonant in Arabic and must be pronounced clearly whether it occurs at the beginning, middle or end of a word.

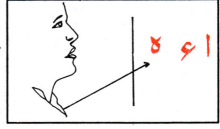

The letter, Ha' (ه) is pronounced from the same part of the throat, but it emerges from a slightly higher point.

الْهَمْزَةِ وَالْهَا أَ ءَ أهْ

3.   Wasatul Halq – (2) وَسَطُ الْحَلْقِ

Middle of the throat is the *makhraj* of ع ('Ain), and just above it, ح (hâ), a sharper "h" sound than ---- is pronounced.

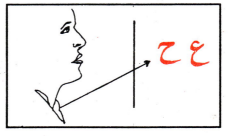

العَين والحَاء أَحْ أَعْ

4.   Adnâ al-Halq – (2) أَدْنَى الْحَلْقِ

The nearest (Front) part of the throat (to the mouth) is the Makhraj of غ (Ghain), and immediately above it emanates خ
The Aqsa (back) has been mentioned first because the sound emanates from the inside and moves toward the front of mouth.

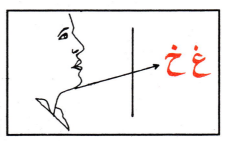

الغَين والخَاء أَخْ أَغْ

---

1   A common error in the pronunciation of ghayn and khâ is caused by allowing them to emerge from the mouth rather than the throat.

(18) حُرُوْفُ اللِّسَان C. Al-Lisaan (Tongue) Letters

The **tongue** is the most important organ for speech production. This is even used as synonymous to language. "If you can control your tongue, you can achieve many things" can be used to mean different things. The tongue is an extremely moveable mass of muscular tissue attached to the floor of the mouth, and is capable of assuming a great variety of positions in the articulation of both vowels and consonants. Having no obvious natural divisions, the surface of the tongue is arbitrarily divided into **four** main parts: the **tip**, the blade, the **front**, and the **back**.

The tongue contains **ten** *makhârij* for **eighteen** letters. They are also mentioned as *twarfe lisan* letters.

5. اَقْصَى اللِّسَانِ قَرِيْبًا مِنَ الْحَلْقِ

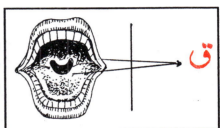

The innermost part (back) of the tongue (i.e., its root) next to the throat along with corresponding upper part of roof of the mouth near **uvula** (pendant fleshy lobe) is the *makhraj* of ق (*Qâf*) . (اَقْ) Aq. (Qalb قَلْب = heart).

6. اَقْصَى اللِّسَانِ قَرِيْبًا مِنَ الْفَمِ

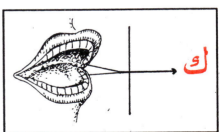

The innermost part of the tongue toward the mouth and what corresponds to it from the roof of the mouth is *makhraj* (point of articulation) of ك (*kâf*) . It is a little more toward the front of the tongue than ق

(اَكْ) Ak (Kalb كَلْب = dog).

7. Wasatul Lisân الجِيْم وَالشِّيْن وَالْيَاءِ: وَسَطُ اللِّسَان

The middle of the tongue and the corresponding upper surface (------- ---) of the roof (palate) of the mouth is the *makhraj* of ج (*Jîm*) . ش (*Shîn*) , and ى (*yâ*) which is either *Layyinah* or *Mutaharrik*, (i.e., when it begins a syllable as the consonant "y". These are also called *Hurufe Shajaria* for coming out of the body of the tongue – i.e., Munfatihah. Pronounce: (اَجْ, اَشْ, اَرْ)

8. ض Dhâd Hâffatul Lisân: حَافَّةِ اللِّسَان

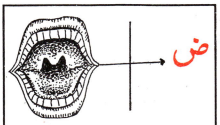

One or both edges of the tongue along with the upper back molar teeth (more often and more easily on the left side of the tongue) is the *makhraj* of ض (dhâd). It is pronounced heavy. اَضَ Adh.

9. (lâm) ل Hâffatul Lisân : حَافَّةُ اللِّسَانُ

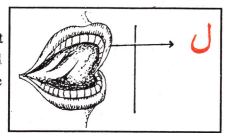

(From the tip (between the edge) of the tongue (usually the right side) and the gums of the upper front molars, canine teeth and incisors is the makhraj of ل (Lâm), e.g., (Al) اَل = the (definite article).

10. Nûn Taraful Lisân النون : طَرَفِ اللِّسَان

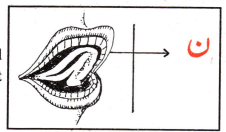

Between the tip of the tongue and the gums of the two upper central incisors is the *Makhraj* of ن (Nûn). It is pronounced from just inside the *makhraj* of ل (lâm), e.g., An اَنْ = to, that, if.

11. Raa: Taraful Lisân الراء : طَرَفِ اللِّسَان

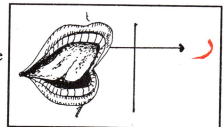

Between the upper part of the tip of the tongue and the gums of the two upper central incisors is the *makhraj* of ر (Râ), e.g., اَرْ Ar.

12. التاء والطاء والدال : ظهر اللسان

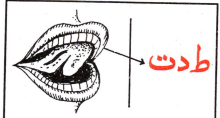

The tip of the tongue and the root of the upper incisor teeth is the makhraj of ط (Tâ'), د (dâl), and ت (tâ). اَتُ , اَطُ , اَدُ.

13. الزاى والصاد والسين : راس اللسان

The tip of the tongue near the inner plates of the upper central incisors is the makhraj of ص (sâd), س (sîn) and ز (za). In pronouncing these letters, the air is exhaled in a soft blow. If the exhalation is not continued, the pronunciation will not be correct.

س sound is identical with the English s as in so.

ز sound is identical with the English z as in zone.

ص Sound is almost identical with the English s in sauce or source.

14. ظهرُاللسان Zahrul Lisân : الثاء، والظاء، والذال

Between the upper surface of the tongue near the end and the tips of the two upper central incisors is the *makhraj* of ظ (zâ), ذ (dhâl) and ث (thâ). And they are called *hurufe lithawyah.* أَثْ، أَذْ، أَظْ

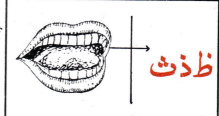

ث Sound is almost identical with the English th sound in the word thin.

ذ Sound is identical with the English th sound in the word that.

ظ Zoa belongs to velarized consonants, i.e., When it is articulated, the back of the tongue is raised more to fit into the concavity or soft palate.

D. Shafawi Letters اَلْحُرُوفُ الشَّفَوِيَّة

15. ف (Fâ) – الشفة السفلى

Between the inside of the lower lip and the tips of the upper incisors is the makhraj of ف (fâ). أَفْ

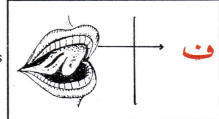

16. الباء، والميم، والواو : الشفتان

Between the two lips is the *makhraj* of ب (bâ), م (mîm) and و (waw) Layyinah or Mutaharrick (i.e., when it begins a syllable as the consonant "w". So they are named *Al-huruf Shafaweya.* أَبْ، أَمْ، أَوْ

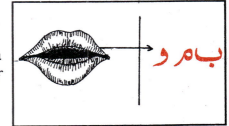

E. The Nasal Passage ....

17. *Khayshumi* (Nasal) Letters – حُرُوفُ الْخَيْشُومْ

The nasal passage is the *makhraj* of غُنَّـة (*Al-Ghunnah*). It is not a letter, but a quality belonging to the letter ن (nûn) and م (mîm), a sound coming from the nose in which the tongue has no part.

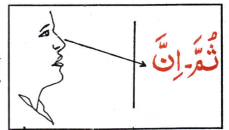

THE DECLARATION OF FAITH (ÎMÂN) ایمان

کلمہ طیبہ
1.   **The code of Holy creed (Kalimah Tayyiba)**

لَآ اِلَهَ اِلَّا اللهُ مُحَمَّدٌ رَّسُوْلُ اللهِ۔

کلمہ شہادت
2.   **The code of justifying (Kalimah Shahâdat)**

اَشْهَدُ اَنْ لَّا اِلَهَ اِلَّا اللهُ وَحْدَهُ لَاشَرِيْكَ لَهُ وَاَشْهَدُ اَنَّ مُحَمَّدًا عَبْدُهُ وَرَسُوْلُهُ۔

کلمہ تمجید
3.   **The code of exaltation (Kalimah Tamjeed)**

سُبْحَانَ اللهِ وَالْحَمْدُ لِلهِ وَلَا اِلَهَ اِلَّا اللهُ وَاللهُ اَكْبَرُ وَلَاحَوْلَ وَلَاقُوَّةَ اِلَّا بِاللهِ الْعَلِيِّ الْعَظِيْمِ

کلمہ توحید
4.   **The code of the unity of God (Kalimah Tauhîd)**

لَآ اِلَهَ اِلَّا اللهُ وَحْدَهُ لَاشَرِيْكَ لَهُ لَهُ الْمُلْكُ وَلَهُ الْحَمْدُ يُحْيِىْ وَيُمِيْتُ وَهُوَ حَيٌّ لَّايَمُوْتُ اَبَدًا اَبَدًا ذُوالْجَلَالِ وَالْاِكْرَامِ بِيَدِهِ الْخَيْرُ وَهُوَعَلَى كُلِّ شَىْءٍ قَدِيْرٌ۔

5.   **The code of Glorifying (Kalimah Tahmîd)**

کلمہ تحمید

سُبْحَانَ اللهِ وَبِحَمْدِهِ سُبْحَانَ اللهِ الْعَلِيِّ الْعَظِيْمِ وَبِحَمْدِهِ اَسْتَغْفِرُ اللهَ رَبِّيْ مِنْ كُلِّ ذَنْبٍ وَّاَتُوْبُ اِلَيْهِ۔

6. **The code of Repudiating In fidelity (*Kalimah Radde Kufr*)**

اَللّٰهُمَّ اِنِّىْ اَعُوْذُبِكَ مِنْ اَنْ اُشْرِكَ بِكَ شَيْئًا وَّ اَنَا اَعْلَمُ بِهٖ وَ اَسْتَغْفِرُكَ لِمَا لَآ اَعْلَمُ بِهٖ تُبْتُ عَنْهُ وَتَبَرَّاْتُ مِنَ الْكُفْرِ وَالشِّرْكِ وَالْمَعَاصِىْ كُلِّهَا وَاَسْلَمْتُ وَاٰمَنْتُ وَاَقُوْلُ لَآ اِلٰهَ اِلَّا اللهُ مُحَمَّدٌ رَّسُوْلُ اللهِ ؕ

~~~~~~

THE CARDINAL ARTICLES OF FAITH

1. **Imân-e-Mufassal (*Faith in Detail*)**

اِیْمَانِ مُفَصَّل

اٰمَنْتُ بِاللهِ وَ مَلَآئِكَتِهٖ وَكُتُبِهٖ وَرُسُلِهٖ وَالْيَوْمِ الْاٰخِرِ وَ الْقَدَرِ خَيْرِهٖ وَشَرِّهٖ مِنَ اللهِ تَعَالٰى وَالْبَعْثِ بَعْدَ الْمَوْتِ

2. **Îmân-e-Mujmal (*Faith in Brief*)**

اِیْمَانِ مُجْمَل

اٰمَنْتُ بِاللهِ كَمَا هُوَ بِاَسْمَآئِهٖ وَ صِفَاتِهٖ وَقَبِلْتُ جَمِيْعَ اَحْكَامِهٖ اِقْرَارٌ بِاللِّسَانِ وَ تَصْدِيْقٌ بِالْقَلْبِ

AZÂN (Call for Prayer)

Allâhu Akbar,   Allâh is the Greatest.

اَللهُ اَكْبَرُ اَللهُ اَكْبَرُ ۚ اَللهُ اَكْبَرُ اَللهُ اَكْبَرُ

Ash-hadu-al-Lâilâha Illallâh.
I bear witness that there is none worthy of being worshipped but Allâh.

اَشْهَدُ اَنْ لَّا اِلٰهَ اِلَّا اللهُ ۚ اَشْهَدُ اَنْ لَّا اِلٰهَ اِلَّا اللهُ

Ash-hadu Anna Muhammadar Rasûlallâh,
I bear witness that Muhammad is the Apostle of Allâh.

اَشْهَدُ اَنَّ مُحَمَّدًا رَّسُوْلُ اللهِ ۚ اَشْهَدُ اَنَّ مُحَمَّدًا رَّسُوْلُ اللهِ

Hayya 'Alas-salâh,   Come to Prayer.

حَيَّ عَلَى الصَّلٰوةِ ۚ حَيَّ عَلَى الصَّلٰوةِ ۚ

Hayya Alal Falâh, Come to Success.

حَيَّ عَلَى الْفَلَاحِ ۚ حَيَّ عَلَى الْفَلَاحِ ۚ

Allâhu Akbar,   Allâh is the Greatest.

اَللهُ اَكْبَرُ اَللهُ اَكْبَرُ

Lâ-ilâha Illallâh,   There is none worthy of being worshipped but Allâh.

لَا اِلٰهَ اِلَّا اللهُ

(In Azân for Fajr Salâh the following sentence is added.)

As-salâtu Khairum Minan Nawm,   Salat is better than sleep.

اَلصَّلٰوةُ خَيْرٌ مِّنَ النَّوْمِ ۚ اَلصَّلٰوةُ خَيْرٌ مِّنَ النَّوْمِ ۚ

(After Azân when the Muslim are assembled at the place of worship these sentences are recited.)

Prayer has indeed started. Qad Qamatis-Salâh

قَدْ قَامَتِ الصَّلٰوةُ ۚ قَدْ قَامَتِ الصَّلٰوةُ ۚ

DU'Â AFTER AZÂN دُعَا بَعْدِ اذَان

اَللّٰهُمَّ رَبَّ هٰذِهِ الدَّعْوَةِ التَّامَّةِ وَالصَّلٰوةِ الْقَآئِمَةِ اٰتِ مُحَمَّدَا ِالْوَسِيْلَةَ وَالْفَضِيْلَةَ وَالدَّرَجَةَ الرَّفِيْعَةَ وَابْعَثْهُ مَقَامًا مَّحْمُوْدَا ِالَّذِيْ وَعَدْتَّهٗ وَارْزُقْنَا شَفَاعَتَهٗ يَوْمَ الْقِيٰمَةِ اِنَّكَ لَا تُخْلِفُ الْمِيْعَادَ

84

PRAYER (Salât) صلوٰۃ (نماز)

1. **Exaltation Recited after the first *Takbir* for prayer**

   (*Thana*)

   ثَنَاءٌ بَعْدِ تَكْبِيرِ اَوَّل

   سُبْحٰنَكَ اللّٰهُمَّ وَبِحَمْدِكَ وَتَبَارَكَ اسْمُكَ وَتَعَالٰى جَدُّكَ وَلَآ اِلٰهَ غَيْرُكَ ۚ

2. **Exaltation [*Thana*] in Bowing (*Ruku'*)**

   تَسْبِيحِ رُكُوْع

   سُبْحَانَ رَبِّيَ الْعَظِيمِ ۚ

3. **Prayer said when standing from *Ruku'* (*Qiyâm*)**

   دُعَاءٌ وَقْتِ قِيَامِ رُكُوْع

   سَمِعَ اللّٰهُ لِمَنْ حَمِدَهٗ ۚ رَبَّنَا لَكَ الْحَمْدُ ۚ

4. **Exaltation in the obedience (*Sajdah*)**

   تَسْبِيحِ سُجُوْد

   سُبْحَانَ رَبِّيَ الْاَعْلٰى ۚ

5. **Salutation to Allâh**

   Tashahhud (Attahiyyât). اَلتَّحِيَّاتُ

   اَلتَّحِيَّاتُ لِلّٰهِ وَالصَّلَوٰتُ وَالطَّيِّبٰتُ ۚ اَلسَّلَامُ عَلَيْكَ اَيُّهَا النَّبِيُّ وَ رَحْمَةُ اللّٰهِ وَبَرَكَاتُهٗ ۚ اَلسَّلَامُ عَلَيْنَا وَعَلٰى عِبَادِ اللّٰهِ الصّٰلِحِينَ ۚ اَشْهَدُ اَنْ لَّا اِلٰهَ اِلَّا اللّٰهُ وَاَشْهَدُ اَنَّ مُحَمَّدًا عَبْدُهٗ وَرَسُوْلُهٗ ۝

اَللّٰهُمَّ صَلِّ عَلٰى مُحَمَّدٍ وَّعَلٰى اٰلِ مُحَمَّدٍ كَمَا صَلَّيْتَ عَلٰى اِبْرَاهِيْمَ وَعَلٰى اٰلِ اِبْرَاهِيْمَ اِنَّكَ حَمِيْدٌ مَّجِيْدٌ ؕ اَللّٰهُمَّ بَارِكْ عَلٰى مُحَمَّدٍ وَّعَلٰى اٰلِ مُحَمَّدٍ كَمَا بَارَكْتَ عَلٰى اِبْرَاهِيْمَ وَعَلٰى اٰلِ اِبْرَاهِيْمَ اِنَّكَ حَمِيْدٌ مَّجِيْدٌ ۰

Du'a-e-Masûrah دُعَائے مَاثُوْرَه

اَللّٰهُمَّ اغْفِرْلِيْ وَلِوَالِدَىَّ وَالْجَمِيْعِ الْمُؤْمِنِيْنَ وَالْمُؤْمِنٰتِ وَالْمُسْلِمِيْنَ وَالْمُسْلِمَاتِ الْاَحْيَاءِ مِنْهُمْ وَالْاَمْوَاتِ اِنَّكَ مُجِيْبُ الدَّعَوَاتِ بِرَحْمَتِكَ يَا اَرْحَمَ الرّٰحِمِيْنَ ؕ

Salâm سَلَام

اَلسَّلَامُ عَلَيْكُمْ وَرَحْمَةُ اللّٰهِ ۚ

Du'a-e-Qunût دُعَائے قُنُوْت

اَللّٰهُمَّ اِنَّا نَسْتَعِيْنُكَ وَنَسْتَغْفِرُكَ وَنُؤْمِنُ بِكَ وَنَتَوَكَّلُ عَلَيْكَ وَنُثْنِى عَلَيْكَ الْخَيْرَ ۫ وَنَشْكُرُكَ وَلَا نَكْفُرُكَ وَنَخْلَعُ وَنَتْرُكُ مَنْ يَّفْجُرُكَ اَللّٰهُمَّ اِيَّاكَ نَعْبُدُ وَلَكَ نُصَلِّىْ وَنَسْجُدُ وَاِلَيْكَ نَسْعٰى وَنَحْفِدُ وَنَرْجُوْ رَحْمَتَكَ وَنَخْشٰى عَذَابَكَ اِنَّ عَذَابَكَ بِالْكُفَّارِ مُلْحِقٌ ۰

Funeral [Janazah] Du'a

دُعَائے جنازَہ

اَللّٰهُمَّ اغْفِرْ لِحَيِّنَا وَمَيِّتِنَا وَشَاهِدِنَا وَغَائِبِنَا وَصَغِيْرِنَا وَكَبِيْرِنَا وَذَكَرِنَا وَاُنْثَانَا، اَللّٰهُمَّ مَنْ اَحْيَيْتَهٗ مِنَّا فَاَحْيِهٖ عَلَى الْاِسْلَامِ وَمَنْ تَوَفَّيْتَهٗ مِنَّا فَتَوَفَّهٗ عَلَى الْاِيْمَانِ ۟

Qabr Visitation Du'a

قَبْرِسْتَان مِیں دَاخِل هُونے کی دُعَا

اَلسَّلَامُ عَلَيْكُمْ يَا اَهْلَ الْقُبُوْرِ مِنَ الْمُسْلِمِيْنَ وَالْمُؤْمِنِيْنَ. اَنْتُمْ لَنَا سَلَفٌ وَّنَحْنُ لَكُمْ تَبَعٌ وَّاِنَّا اِنْشَاءَ اللّٰهُ بِكُمْ لَاحِقُوْنَ. يَرْحَمُ اللّٰهُ الْمُسْتَقْدِمِيْنَ مِنَّا وَالْمُسْتَاْخِرِيْنَ نَسْئَلُ اللّٰهَ تَعَالٰى اَنْ يَّرْحَمَنَا وَاِيَّاكُمْ. اٰمِيْن

Qurbani (Sacrifice) Du'a

نِیَّتِ قُرْبانی

اِنِّيْ وَجَّهْتُ وَجْهِيَ لِلَّذِيْ فَطَرَ السَّمٰوٰتِ وَالْاَرْضَ حَنِيْفًا وَّمَا اَنَا مِنَ الْمُشْرِكِيْنَ ۞ اِنَّ صَلَاتِيْ وَنُسُكِيْ وَمَحْيَايَ وَمَمَاتِيْ لِلّٰهِ رَبِّ الْعٰلَمِيْنَ ۞ لَاشَرِيْكَ لَهٗ وَبِذٰلِكَ اُمِرْتُ وَاَنَا مِنَ الْمُسْلِمِيْنَ ۞ اَللّٰهُمَّ تَقَبَّلْ مِنِّيْ هٰذِهِ الْاُضْحِيَّةَ كَمَا تَقَبَّلْتَ مِنْ اِبْرٰهِيْمَ خَلِيْلِكَ وَاِسْمٰعِيْلَ ذَبِيْحِكَ وَمُحَمَّدٍ نَبِيِّكَ وَمُصْطَفَاكَ صَلَّى اللّٰهُ عَلَيْهِ وَسَلَّمَ اَللّٰهُمَّ مِنْكَ وَلَكَ بِسْمِ اللّٰهِ اللّٰهُ اَكْبَرُ ۔

Put all names of persons sacrificing. جس کی طرف سے قربانی ہو جاری ہو اس کا پورا نام ادا کریں۔

اَللّٰهُمَّ هٰذِهٖ عَقِيْقَةُ ابْنِیْ فُلَانٍ دَمُهَا بِدَمِهٖ وَلَحْمُهَا بِلَحْمِهٖ وَ عَظْمُهَا بِعَظْمِهٖ وَجِلْدُهَا بِجِلْدِهٖ وَشَعْرُهَا بِشَعْرِهٖ اَللّٰهُمَّ اجْعَلْهَا فِدَآءً لِّابْنِیْ مِنَ النَّارِ اِنِّیْ وَجَّهْتُ وَجْهِیَ لِلَّذِیْ فَطَرَ السَّمٰوٰتِ وَالْاَرْضَ حَنِيْفًا وَّمَآ اَنَا مِنَ الْمُشْرِكِيْنَ اِنَّ صَلَوٰتِیْ وَنُسُكِیْ وَمَحْيَایَ وَمَمَاتِیْ لِلّٰهِ رَبِّ الْعٰلَمِيْنَ لَا شَرِيْكَ لَهٗ وَبِذَالِكَ اُمِرْتُ وَاَنَا مِنَ الْمُسْلِمِيْنَ ۚ اَللّٰهُمَّ مِنْكَ وَلَكَ ۚ پھر اللهُ اَكْبَرُ ۚ

بچّے کا پورا نام یہاں ادا کریں۔

Put actual name of the child here.

AHADITH-E-NABAWI (SAW)

KNOWLEDGE علم

طَلَبُ الْعِلْمِ فَرِيْضَةٌ عَلَى كُلِّ مُسْلِمٍ وَّمُسْلِمَةٍ :

Seeking knowledge is Fard (obligatory) for every Muslim, male and female.

مَنْ خَرَجَ لِطَلَبِ الْعِلْمِ فَهُوَ كَفَّارَةٌ لِّمَا مَضَى :

Whoever goes out for knowledge, his past (sins) are effaced.

تَدَارُسُ الْعِلْمِ سَاعَةً مِّنَ اللَّيْلِ خَيْرٌ مِّنْ اِحْيَائِهَا :

Study for knowledge for an hour at night is better than wake up all night.

اُطْلُبُوا الْعِلْمَ وَلَوْ كَانَ فِى الصِّيْنِ :   اُطْلُبِ الْعِلْمَ مِنَ الْمَهْدِ اِلَى اللَّحْدِ :

Seek knowledge from cradle to grave.   Seek Knowledge even it be in China.

اَلْمَاهِرُ بِالْقُرْاٰنِ مَعَ السَّفَرَةِ الْبَرَرَةِ الْكِرَامِ وَالَّذِىْ يَقْرَءُ الْقُرْاٰنَ وَيَتَعْتَعُ

فِيْهِ وَهُوَ عَلَيْهِ شَاقٌّ فَلَهٗ اَجْرَانِ :

وَلَا تَعْقِقْ وَالِدَيْكَ وَاِنْ اَمَرَكَ اَنْ تَخْرُجَ مِنْ اَهْلِكَ وَمَالِكَ :

كُلُّ الذُّنُوْبِ يَغْفِرُ اللهُ تَعَالٰى مِنْهَا مَا شَاءَ اِلَّا عُقُوْقُ الْوَالِدَيْنِ

فَاِنَّهٗ يُعَجِّلُ لِصَاحِبِهٖ فِى الْحَيَاةِ قَبْلَ الْمَمَاتِ :

Allâh may forgive all sins if He wishes except one annoys the parents. So he will be rushed to his companions in this life before death.

Modesty is the part of branch of Faith.   اَلْحَيَاءُ شُعْبَةٌ مِّنَ الْاِيْمَانِ :

The Paradise lies under the feet of your mother.   اِنَّ الْجَنَّةَ تَحْتَ اَقْدَامِ اُمَّهَاتِكُمْ :

DIFFERENT SIGNS IN THE QUR'ÂN

At the end of an ayah along with the stop sign there are additional signs. Some of these are listed below along with the usage.

Stop

     ○   Means end of an ayah.

     مـ̥   or مـ   means a compulsory stop, known as Waqfe Lâzim.

     قف̥   or قف   means a pause.

Stop Preferred

     ط̥   or ط

     ج̥   Or ج

No Stop

     لا̥   or لا   means do not stop if it occurs in the middle of an ayah. If it occurs at the end of an ayah, it means no stop is preferred.

No Stop Preferred

     نا̥   Or ن

     صلى̥   Or صلى

     ص̥   Or ص

Some other common signs: Ruku' ع = ركوع ; Juz or Portion جزء ; Sajdah سجدة at this sign you must perform Sajdah before continuing your recitation.

MAKING A STOP (PAUSE)

It should be explained to the child that a letter followed by any of the following signs with a vowel mark, should be made *Sâkin* after joining it with the letter before it (dropping vowel marks). If there are no vowel marks, and there is a *Sukûn* (*Jazm*), it will remain the same. Round 'Ta' will be replaced by 'Ha'. Long 'Ta' will not be replaced by 'Ha'. Lone *Alif*, after two *Fatha* (*Zabar*) will be read, but only as if it had one *Fatha* (*Zabar*). If there is only one *Fatha* (*Zabar*) before *Alif*, it will remain as is. A lone 'Ya', after two *Fatha* (*Zabar*), will change into an *Alif*. In smaller type, the pronunciation of each example has been written below it.

نیچے کو سمجھائیں کہ جس حرف کے نیچے کی نشانیوں میں سے کوئی نشانی آجائے اور وہ حرف حرکت والا ہو تو اس کے زیر یا زبر یا پیش کو کالعدم سمجھ کر اس کے ساتھ اس کے پہلے حرف کو ملا کر ساکن کر دیں اگر متحرک نہیں تو بلکہ اس پر جزم ہے تو وہی صورت رہے گی گول تے ہے سے بدل جائے گی لمبی تے ہے سے نہیں بدلے گی دو زبر کے بعد جو خالی الف ہے وہ پڑھا جائے گا۔ اور صرف ایک زبر پڑھا جائے گا اگر الف سے پہلے ایک زبر ہے تو وہی صورت رہے گی۔ دو زبر کے بعد خالی یے الف سے بدل جائے گی۔ باریک قلم سے ہر ایک کی مثال کے نیچے اس کا تلفظ درج کیا گیا ہے۔

علامت وقف مطلق ط	علامت وقف جائز ج	علامت وقف لازم م	علامت آیت ○
دَلْوَةٌ	غَيْرُهٗ	وَالِدَتِكَ	رُسُلْ
دَلْوَة	غَيْرِهٗ	وَالِدَتِكْ	رُسُلْ
عَظِيْمٌ	صٰدِقِيْنَ	فَنَسِىَ	حَافِظٌ هُوَ
عَظِيْم	صٰدِقِيْن	فَنَسِیٰ	حَافِظْ هُوْ
شَكُوْرٌ	تَعْلَمُوْنَ	يُنْفِقُوْنَ	فِيْهِ شَىْءٌ
شَكُوْر	تَعْلَمُوْن	يُنْفِقُوْن	فِيْهِ شَىْءْ
شُهَدَآءٌ	زَوْجَيْنِ	ضَلَلْ	أُمُوْرٌ اَلْبَابُ
شُهَدَآء	زَوْجَيْن	ضَلَلْ	أُمُوْر اَلْبَابْ
مُصَلًّى	ضُحٰى	رَقِيْبًا	عِبَادِهِ الْعُلَمٰؤُا
مُصَلًّا	ضُحَا	رَقِيْبَا	عِبَادِهِ الْعُلَمٰءْ
تَنْهَرْ	كُوِّرَتْ	ثَمٰنِيَةٌ	أَبِى قُوَّةٌ
تَنْهَرْ	كُوِّرَتْ	ثَمٰنِيَهْ	اَبْ قُوَّة

(۱) سُوْرَةُ الْفَاتِحَةِ مَکِّیَّةٌ (۵)

بِسْمِ اللهِ الرَّحْمٰنِ الرَّحِیْمِ

اَلْحَمْدُ لِلّٰهِ رَبِّ الْعٰلَمِیْنَ ۝ الرَّحْمٰنِ الرَّحِیْمِ ۝ مٰلِكِ

یَوْمِ الدِّیْنِ ۝ اِیَّاكَ نَعْبُدُ وَاِیَّاكَ نَسْتَعِیْنُ ۝

اِهْدِنَا الصِّرَاطَ الْمُسْتَقِیْمَ ۝ صِرَاطَ الَّذِیْنَ

اَنْعَمْتَ عَلَیْهِمْ ۙ غَیْرِ الْمَغْضُوْبِ عَلَیْهِمْ

وَلَا الضَّآلِّیْنَ ۝

آیَةُ الْکُرْسِیْ

اَللهُ لَاۤ اِلٰهَ اِلَّا هُوَ ۚ اَلْحَیُّ الْقَیُّوْمُ ۚ لَا تَأْخُذُهٗ سِنَةٌ

وَّلَا نَوْمٌ ۚ لَهٗ مَا فِی السَّمٰوٰتِ وَمَا فِی الْاَرْضِ ۗ

مَنْ ذَا الَّذِیْ یَشْفَعُ عِنْدَهٗۤ اِلَّا بِاِذْنِهٖ ۚ یَعْلَمُ مَا

بَيْنَ اَيْدِيْهِمْ وَمَا خَلْفَهُمْ ۚ وَلَا يُحِيْطُوْنَ بِشَىْءٍ

مِّنْ عِلْمِهٖۤ اِلَّا بِمَا شَآءَ ۚ وَسِعَ كُرْسِيُّهُ السَّمٰوٰتِ وَ

الْاَرْضَ ۚ وَلَا يَـُٔوْدُهٗ حِفْظُهُمَا ۚ وَهُوَ الْعَلِيُّ الْعَظِيْمُ ۲۵۵

بِسْمِ اللّٰهِ الرَّحْمٰنِ الرَّحِيْمِ

قُلْ يٰۤاَيُّهَا الْكٰفِرُوْنَ ۙ۱ لَاۤ اَعْبُدُ مَا تَعْبُدُوْنَ ۙ۲ وَلَاۤ

اَنْتُمْ عٰبِدُوْنَ مَاۤ اَعْبُدُ ۚ۳ وَلَاۤ اَنَا عَابِدٌ مَّا عَبَدْتُّمْ ۙ۴ وَلَاۤ

اَنْتُمْ عٰبِدُوْنَ مَاۤ اَعْبُدُ ۭ۵ لَكُمْ دِيْنُكُمْ وَلِيَ دِيْنِ ۧ۶

بِسْمِ اللّٰهِ الرَّحْمٰنِ الرَّحِيْمِ

اِذَا جَآءَ نَصْرُ اللّٰهِ وَالْفَتْحُ ۙ۱ وَرَاَيْتَ النَّاسَ

يَدْخُلُوْنَ فِىْ دِيْنِ اللّٰهِ اَفْوَاجًا ۙ۝ فَسَبِّحْ بِحَمْدِ

رَبِّكَ وَاسْتَغْفِرْهُ ؕ اِنَّهٗ كَانَ تَوَّابًا ۝

بِسْمِ اللّٰهِ الرَّحْمٰنِ الرَّحِیْمِ

تَبَّتْ يَدَآ اَبِىْ لَهَبٍ وَّتَبَّ ۝ مَاۤ اَغْنٰى عَنْهُ مَالُهٗ وَمَا

كَسَبَ ۝ سَيَصْلٰى نَارًا ذَاتَ لَهَبٍ ۙ۝ وَّامْرَاَتُهٗ ؕ

حَمَّالَةَ الْحَطَبِ ۝ فِىْ جِیْدِهَا حَبْلٌ مِّنْ مَّسَدٍ ۝

بِسْمِ اللّٰهِ الرَّحْمٰنِ الرَّحِیْمِ

قُلْ هُوَ اللّٰهُ اَحَدٌ ۚ۝ اَللّٰهُ الصَّمَدُ ۚ۝ لَمْ يَلِدْ ۙ۬ وَلَمْ

يُوْلَدْ ۙ۝ وَلَمْ يَكُنْ لَّهٗ كُفُوًا اَحَدٌ ۝

سُوْرَةُ الْفَلَقِ مَكِّيَّةٌ (٢٠) (١١٣) اٰیَاتُهَا ٥ رُكُوْعُهَا ١

بِسْمِ اللهِ الرَّحْمٰنِ الرَّحِيْمِ

قُلْ اَعُوْذُ بِرَبِّ الْفَلَقِ ۞ مِنْ شَرِّ مَا خَلَقَ ۞ وَ مِنْ شَرِّ غَاسِقٍ اِذَا وَقَبَ ۞ وَمِنْ شَرِّ النَّفّٰثٰتِ فِی الْعُقَدِ ۞ وَمِنْ شَرِّ حَاسِدٍ اِذَا حَسَدَ ۞

سُوْرَةُ النَّاسِ مَكِّيَّةٌ (٢١) (١١٤) اٰیَاتُهَا ٦ رُكُوْعُهَا ١

بِسْمِ اللهِ الرَّحْمٰنِ الرَّحِيْمِ

قُلْ اَعُوْذُ بِرَبِّ النَّاسِ ۞ مَلِكِ النَّاسِ ۞ اِلٰهِ النَّاسِ ۞ مِنْ شَرِّ الْوَسْوَاسِ ۞ الْخَنَّاسِ ۞ الَّذِیْ یُوَسْوِسُ فِیْ صُدُوْرِ النَّاسِ ۞ مِنَ الْجِنَّةِ وَالنَّاسِ ۞

تَبٰرَكَ الَّخ

HOLY NAMES OF ALLÂH SUBHÂNAHU WA T'ÂLA

أَسْمَاءُ الْحُسْنٰى لِلّٰهِ تَعَالٰى عَزَّ اسْمُهُ

بِسْمِ اللهِ الرَّحْمٰنِ الرَّحِيمِ

هُوَ اللهُ الَّذِى لَا اِلٰهَ اِلَّا			الرَّحْمٰن	الرَّحِيم	الْمَلِك	الْقُدُّوس	السَّلَام
الْمُؤْمِن	الْمُهَيْمِن	الْعَزِيز	الْجَبَّار	الْمُتَكَبِّر	الْخَالِق	الْبَارِئ	الْمُصَوِّر
الْغَفَّار	الْقَهَّار	الْوَهَّاب	الرَّزَّاق	الْفَتَّاح	الْعَلِيم	الْقَابِض	الْبَاسِط
الْخَافِض	الرَّافِع	الْمُعِزّ	الْمُذِلّ	السَّمِيع	الْبَصِير	الْحَكَم	الْعَدْل
اللَّطِيف	الْخَبِير	الْحَلِيم	الْعَظِيم	الْغَفُور	الشَّكُور	الْعَلِيّ	الْكَرِيم
الْحَفِيظ	الْمُقِيت	الْحَسِيب	الْجَلِيل	الْكَرِيم	الرَّقِيب	الْمُجِيب	الْوَاسِع
الْحَكِيم	الْوَدُود	الْمَجِيد	الْبَاعِث	الشَّهِيد	الْحَقّ	الْوَكِيل	الْقَوِيّ
الْمَتِين	الْوَلِيّ	الْحَمِيد	الْمُحْصِى	الْمُبْدِى	الْمُعِيد	الْمُحْيِى	الْمُمِيت
الْحَىّ	الْقَيُّوم	الْوَاجِد	الْمَاجِد	الْوَاحِد	الْاَحَد	الصَّمَد	الْقَادِر
الْمُقْتَدِر	الْمُقَدِّم	الْمُؤَخِّر	الْاَوَّل	الْاٰخِر	الظَّاهِر	الْبَاطِن	الْوَالِى
الْمُتَعَالِى	الْبَرّ	التَّوَّاب	الْمُنْتَقِم	الْعَفُوّ	الرَّؤُوف	مَالِكُ الْمُلْك	
ذُو الْجَلَالِ وَالْاِكْرَام		الْجَامِع	الْمُقْسِط	الْغَنِىّ	الْمُغْنِى	الْمَانِع	الضَّارّ
النَّافِع	النُّور	الْهَادِى	الْبَدِيع	الْبَاقِى	الْوَارِث	الرَّشِيد	الصَّبُور
			الشَّكُور	الْمُعْطِى			

أَسْمَاءُ اللهِ تَعَالَى الْحُسْنَى الَّتِى أَمَرَنَا بِالدُّعَاءِ بِهَا تِسْعَةٌ وَتِسْعُونَ اِسْمًا مَنْ أَحْصَاهَا دَخَلَ الْجَنَّةَ۔ الْبُخَارِىّ